ANNALS OF THE NEW YORK ACADEMY OF SCIENCES
Volume 260

INSTITUTIONS AND SCIENCE PUBLIC POLICY

Edited by Marion Langer and Doris K. Miller

The New York Academy of Sciences
New York, New York
1975

Copyright, 1975, by The New York Academy of Sciences. All rights reserved. Except for brief quotations by reviewers, reproduction of this publication in whole or in part by any means whatever is strictly prohibited without written permission from the publisher.

Library of Congress Cataloging in Publication Data

```
Main entry under title:

Institutions and science public policy.

    (Annals of the New York Academy of Sciences ;
v. 260)
    Papers of a conference held by the New York Aca-
demy of Sciences, Oct. 17-19, 1974.
    1. Science and state--United States--Congresses.
I. Langer, Marion.  II. Miller, Doris K.
III. New York Academy of Sciences.  IV. Series:
New York Academy of Sciences. Annals ; v. 260.
Q11.N5  vol. 260 [Q127.U6] 508'.1s [353.008'55]
ISBN 0-89072-014-2                      75-33103
```

CCP

Printed in the United States of America

ISBN 0-89072-014-2

ANNOUNCING OF THE NEW YORK ACADEMY OF SCIENCES
VOLUME 260
October 3, 1975

INSTITUTIONS AND SCIENCE PUBLIC POLICY*

Editors and Conference Coorganizers
MARION LANGER AND DORIS K. MILLER

CONTENTS

Introduction. By MARION LANGER AND DORIS K. MILLER	5
Keynote Address: The Incorporation of Science. By HILARY A. ROSE AND STEVEN P. R. ROSE	7

Part I. Science Public Policy as a Function of Government Organization and Political Philosophy

In Search of a National Science Policy. By HAROLD FRUCHTBAUM	32
Public and Private Sector Institutions: Their Interacting Roles in Setting Public Policy. By JOHN FOORD SHERMAN	41
Science and Government: Partners in Science Public Policy. By HOWARD J. LEWIS	53

Part II. Federal and Nonprofit Sector Institutions and Their Influence on Science Public Policy

Foundations and Science Public Policy. By E. CREUTZ AND WAYNE R. GRUNER	62
Academic Institutions' Role, Response, and Requirements under an Effective National Science Policy: or, Who Pays the Piper? By SIDNEY G. ROTH	76
A Critique of Social Science Models of Contemporary Society: A Feminist Perspective. By JUNE NASH	84
The Role of the American Chemical Society re Science Public Policy. By BERNARD S. FRIEDMAN	101
General Discussion	105
Scientists in the Courtroom and the Development of Public Interest Law. By CHARLES HALPERN	111
A Modest Proposal for the Renaissance of Regional Academies of Science. By PHILIP SIEKEVITZ	114
General Discussion	122

* This series of papers is the result of a conference entitled Institutions and Science Public Policy, held by The New York Academy of Sciences on October 17, 18, and 19, 1974.

INTRODUCTION

Marion Langer

American Orthopsychiatric Association
New York, New York 10019

Doris K. Miller

New York State Psychological Association
New York, New York 10019

United States scientists enjoyed generous support from government and industry during two prosperous decades following World War II. Conferences such as this one did not tend to take place in those years. Recently, a spate of conferences has addressed how government science policy is formulated and who has decision-making power over the questions that scientists research and the uses of their output. This contagion of concern seems to have evolved from a confluence of events: certain applications of science and technology in the Vietnam War, President Nixon's dismantling of science advisement bodies, and steadily decreasing government funding of science training and research.

As we had hoped when we organized this meeting, the proceedings that follow reflect a very broad range of views about the interaction of government and science. Additionally, this conference faces the relationship of scientists and their work to political systems. This theme is cogently examined by Hilary and Steven Rose, two English scientists, whose joint keynote speech provides one overseas perspective of United States government and science within the context of a Marxist analysis. Their literate, incisive paper evoked both support and challenge from participants in public, private, nonprofit, and profit sectors. The Roses made a unique contribution to the continuity and integration of sessions by serving as scholars-in-residence, summing up at each day's end the substance of presentations and discussions.

What conclusions can be drawn from these two and a half days of intensive exchange? That scientists differ in their views of the definition, privilege, and responsibilities of scientists; range from deepest pessimism to considerable optimism about the world's future; embrace all positions on the political spectrum and display great variance in their rationalizations of the political and social contradictions within which they do their work. Thus, the proceedings are likely to include analyses or viewpoints both congruent and antithetical to those of each reader. And that characterizes the real world in which scientists, politicians, and the public must hammer out a survival system.

As this publication goes to press it should be noted that Gerald Ford contemplates reinstitution of a President's science advisement body and government critics of the science community are attempting to place control of research in the hands of Congress. How these two moves are resolved may well shape the answers to questions raised in this conference.

The excellence of this meeting is owed to many anonymous people as well as to those whose contributions appear in this publication.

Inexplicably, tapes of the Friday afternoon session, chaired by Dr. Seymour Melman, whose participants came from industry and business, think tanks and unions, never materialized. Since two men in that session, Herbert I. Fusfeld and Frank Collins, heroically stepped in at the eleventh hour, formal papers were not requested of them; the presentation by Daniel Callahan was also not recorded. We apologize to all concerned for this regrettable and irrevocable loss.

KEYNOTE ADDRESS

THE INCORPORATION OF SCIENCE

Hilary A. Rose

*Department of Social Administration
London School of Economics
London WC2, England*

Steven P. R. Rose

*Department of Biology
The Open University
Bucks, England*

Over the last decade we have heard a good deal about the crisis in science. This situation is in some ways like the behavior of Alice's White Queen: In the early days there was more alarm about the *coming* crisis in Western science, than there is now, when economic and political crisis has finally come about. Indeed, scientists have behaved very much like the White Queen, who screamed violently in anticipation of the brooch pricking her finger but who was relatively quiescent when the event finally took place.

However, we would like to distinguish two phases in the debate concerning the crisis in science. The first, crisis I—or the Alice phase—appeared as the *rate* of increase of science spending slackened during the mid-sixties. It was typified by pronouncements such as that of Lord Bowden, Principal of the Manchester Institute of Science and Technology and then Minister of State for Science:

> Processes which have been going on quite steadily for centuries may have to stop ... policies ... may have to be scrapped at great cost in spiritual anguish and perhaps at the price of great economic upheaval. .... All that the government can do about scientific fashions is to deny some of its scientists the funds they want, and if it does this some of these distinguished and important men will fold up their tents like Arabs and as silently steal away.[1]

or by the physicist, Professor Bishop, who in the face of the Labour government's decision not to take part in the proposed multimillion pound extension to the CERN accelerator facilities, wrote:

> It could well be that future historians will single out such decisions as the mark of a new era of mental stagnation, the Dark Ages of the 20th and 21st centuries. What is threatened with extinction, when the needs of pure science are lost sight of, is the continuance of a human adventure in thought ...[2]

The White Queen crisis in science was thus one of expectation. Precrisis science, rather like Imperial Britain up to 1870, had looked forward to limitless expansion. All the map would be colored imperial pink and everyone—every man, woman, child, and dog, as Derek Price reminded us—would eventually become a scientist. Fortunately nothing like this happened.

Crisis II was signalized by the 1969 address to the Biochemical Society in London by Dr. Philip Handler, President of the National Academy of Sciences of the United States. In this talk Handler analyzed the broad social and cultural explanations of what he saw as a growing hostility to science. He spoke of the "mounting hysteria, exaggerating the problem of the, nevertheless quite real, threat of various forms of pollution." He saw this hysteria as emanating from an even wider source of social concern than that which arose over the particular problems posed by the war in Vietnam. As if in response to Theodore Roszak's appeal for the restoration of irrationality and magic, Handler wondered whether the very success of science, particularly in biochemistry, had had some part to play in this international unrest "by stripping life of its magic." As the spokesman for science in the United States, Handler naturally concluded by expressing his anxiety lest these legitimate social concerns should lead to cutbacks in the science budget, as he put it, "lest the urgent should drive out the important."[3]

This second crisis, which is our concern here, is much more complex, and cannot be dismissed as merely the special pleading of a particular interest group. In this second phase profound questions began to be raised about the direction and nature of the scientific culture itself. Was science inevitably to be caught up in the technological horrors of the war in Indochina? in pollution? in overpopulation? in domestic counterinsurgency? in the loss of privacy? This contemporary crisis is one that has both economic and cultural dimensions.

In order to understand crisis II, we have to discuss the social functions of science. At least from the mid-twentieth century onwards, the major form of activities included as "science" has been the generation of knowledge and techniques geared to two broad areas of social existence: production and social control. Production science is economically oriented; conducted in industry, government establishments or even the universities, it is concerned with developing industrial capacity, exploiting new materials, and increasing profitability. Social control science takes two forms; it is related either to defense against potential external enemies, or to the development of techniques for the pacification, manipulation, and control of the indigenous population. Even a cursory examination of the annual "science budgets" of advanced industrial countries such as Britain or the United States makes clear that over the last two decades, between 75 and 90% of the annual total can be embraced under these two heads (77% in Britain in 1974/5; 80% in the United States in the fiscal year 1975). It is true that sometimes they are not readily distinguished (e.g., space and atomic research); sometimes what is social control science so far as government procurement is concerned is production science for the corporations that contract to do it.

Because of this overwhelming orientation in the direction of scientific research and development, science has become ever more closely and directly enmeshed in the machinery of state and government, so that today, we will argue in this paper, a correspondence has developed between the nature of the state and the institutions and content of the science and technology carried out within it. Scientific and technological policy formation is the expression of this correspondence, but its study is hampered by the very fact that the two most crucial sectors, those of production and social control, are characterized by intense secrecy and hence are hidden from view. This has made the global activity of science less visible than its importance deserves. Consequently greater attention has been focused on those areas of academic science that are *not* subsumed within these two categories, areas which, it may still be argued, remain relatively (but only relatively) open, such as molecular biology or possibly high-energy physics. Yet attention to these areas, which occupy only a small proportion of the scientific workforce, lays open the danger of mistaking the part for the whole, and also of misunderstanding the nature of the production of scientific knowledge today. For, at the present time, the dominant mode of production of scientific knowledge has become that of knowledge-as-commodity, as a marketable good with a cash value.

Although the issues raised at this point speak of the social functions of science, these have been far from the concerns of most philosophers, historians, and sociologists whose professional task has been to explain the growth of scientific knowledge. Despite an interest in the 1930s in "externalism," that is, the attempt to provide a sociological explanation for the development of science,[4-6] the dominant paradigm for all three disciplines has been internalist in stance. Scientists were given no social existence; all that mattered were the conjectures and refutations between competing individuals and competing schools. Ideas were thus autonomous, unconnected with the social order. Certain kinds of questions became unasked and unaskable. That modern science was born in late Renaissance Europe and not in early China (which looked in principle a more likely society, as Joseph Needham[7] points out) requires either a sociological explanation involving the level and kind of economic and social development, or an internalist explanation turning on "chance," or on a racist assumption of the inherent intellectual superiority of western man.

However, while mainstream academic theorists of scientific development were internalist, scientists and policy-makers were hurried along by history (and particularly World War II) into a pragmatic externalism. While Popper sought to explain how better theory drove out worse theory, scientists and policy makers were, in a more Napoleonic vein, trying to secure supplies for their armies of research workers, and to plan the best strategies and tactics of advances.

In order to follow the implication of the relations of state and science in the context of the present crisis it is necessary to look in more detail at what the science policy-makers and the academic students of science have been saying over the last few years. Against this background, we can then sketch the development of the state-science correspondence—the incorporation of science, that is—in one capitalist country, Britain. We will then have assembled all the principal strands in the argument over the present nature of science, and will be able to test the proposition that scientific rationality *itself* has something wrong with it, and that it is *inevitably* oppressive.

Science Policy: Pragmatic Externalism

In its present form, the literature of science policy and the interrelations of science and government is a mushroom growth of the last two decades, although most of it draws implicitly or explicitly on Bernal's *Social Functions of Science* published in 1939.[8] Bernal's book was a systematic attempt to develop an "external" analysis of science, based on the Marxist view of the interactive relations of science and society. The dialectic between the two meant that social inputs, mainly in the form of funding, but also in more subtle ways, helped science advance, while the advance of science itself was of both direct and indirect social benefit. It was even possible to calculate the short-term profitability of particular pieces of scientific work. However, for Bernal, the long-term development of science was always in contradiction with capitalism, which deformed it and prevented its truly creative development. Science was, of its nature, progressive and hence the natural ally of socialism. Socialism above all meant planning, the rational and logical development of science for the benefit of the people. Only plan, increase the scale of scientific spending some ten-fold (to the level of that current in the USSR, for example), defeat capitalism, and all would be well. The ideology of what was to become "technoeconomism" began to take shape. In a sense the British Labour Party's election manifesto of 1964, concerning the forging of socialism in the white heat of the technological revolution, was a debased after-echo of Bernal's analysis 25 years previously.[9]

But the real development of science policy studies, especially in the United States, was to postdate Bernal's book by 15 years and Hiroshima and Nagasaki by a decade. The reasons for the concern of policy-makers with science in the late 1950s and 1960s are clear; they are symbolized by the growth of the science budget along its exponential path to the magic 3% of the gross national product in the United States, Soviet Union, and Europe. As politicians attempted to understand, control, and direct this growth, political scientists, from Don K. Price[10] through Gilpin,[11] Barber,[12] and Schooler[13] wrestled with questions of the relationship between knowledge and power. Without Bernal's Marxist perspective, they were compelled to ask where scientists stood among the traditional estates of the realm, and how they had influenced, for instance, defense and foreign policy in the era after 1945.

For the policy-makers, the argument took the implicit (and sometimes explicit) view that it was possible, through the funding of science, to influence the direction and speed of scientific advance. While rarely was this pragmatic externalism so crude as to suggest that the frontiers of knowledge could be extended by the mechanical application of resources to a particular problem, it was nonetheless sought in practice to promote general lines or even to achieve defined goals. The most conspicuous examples of this thinking have been the Kennedy response to Sputnik—an American on the moon within 10 years—and now the cancer and heart programs, or, on a lesser scale, the sickle cell anemia program. During the peak of the high-spending years both technological and pure science projects were dreamed up and sponsored with reckless abandon, so that Greenberg[14] was able to document some of the more notorious projects in pure science, such as the Mohole or the Linear Accelerator; but as the economic climate chilled, a greater financial and scientific caution prevailed. Nonetheless particular areas of pure science have been perceived by both government and industry as integral to their political or economic purpose. Thus, governments have given high-energy physics massive state support for both national and international facilities.

Nor has it been only governments who have argued the unity of science, technology, and social goals; industry has taken a similar approach, as witness Bell Telephone Laboratories' funding of William Shockley's work, which both won him a Nobel Prize and laid the foundations for the commercial exploitation of the transistor and microelectronics. It is not difficult to agree with Salomon's view[15] that "the field of pure research constitutes the extreme case of coincidence between the interests of power and the interests of knowledge."

As the 1960s wore on, the policy-makers and the social scientists, by this time including both political scientists and economists of science, began to explore their unity of interests: how could one assist the other? Both within universities and at national and supranational (e.g., OECD, UNESCO) levels research units were established, working on "science studies," "science of science," "science policy," and "science and government," according to the ideological perspectives within which the questions were to be posed. The emphasis now was on quantification, and, as the increasing costs of science and the inevitable slackening off from the exponential growth phase occurred, attempts to justify expenditure on science by proving its relationship to economic growth. This has been a constant feature, for instance, of British work, from that Carter and Williams[16] to the research done by Freeman's group at Sussex.[17] In the United States, the most conspicuous example was the exercise mounted by the Department of Defense under the name

"Project Hindsight." The problem with much of this work was that despite the fact that it was predominantly empirical, because it was separate from the urgent needs felt by the science policy-makers, scholarly, and abstract from the political situation, it yielded for the most part neither theoretical explanation nor even facts very helpful to policy-making. In the United States, which was the first country to sponsor such research groups, there is evidence of the withdrawal of funding, which suggests that so far as their sponsors were concerned, they failed to deliver the goods.

More general and hence of more theoretical interest was the attempt by Weinberg[18] to articulate the criteria by which specific research proposals were to be assessed. His *Criteria for Scientific Choice,* received with great interest by the scientific and science policy-making community alike (not least because Weinberg was himself both a physicist and also a decision maker), attempted to embrace and balance both internalist and externalist arguments. For example, he proposed that major investments in a given field were correct if that development could nourish other adjacent fields (an argument that was to be used in Britain *against* the expansion of high-energy physics and investment in further accelerators).

In 1974, it is apparent that the achievements of science policy, for all Weinberg's clarity of vision, have been limited. This has been clearly perceived at the political level, as many governments have abandoned the position of "Minister of Science" or "Science Advisor."

The reasons for this cutback are not without interest. Science policy-making has reached something of an impasse; the heady days of scientific expansion itself are now well over. The 1960s and early 1970s saw, as we will discuss in more detail in the case of Britain, the deepening integration of science into the machinery of the state. Where scientific rationality pervades all aspects of social life, there is no longer any need to set science apart and to demand for it a policy as if it had an autonomy, as if biology and physics were to be regarded as something separate from an extension of medicine and agriculture on the one hand and military and industrial development on the other. In this same vein, all those many books entitled *Science and Society* (also including one by authors who should perhaps have known better) are, as Levy-Leblond and Jaubert observe,[19] sociologically incorrect, in that they juxtapose, as autonomous if interacting, scientific and social systems. It would be more accurate, if ponderous, to entitle such studies *Science in Society and Society in Science* and indeed two recent books[15, 20] do precisely this. Salomon's book deals with politics in science and science in politics, whereas Blume's attempts to integrate the sociology of science with the science policy literature in an effort to develop a political sociology of science.

The Unity of Science and Technology

In spite of what many historians, philosophers, and sociologists of science have thought, modern science and technology are indivisible. The particular character of modern science ushered in with the Galilean revolution is precisely that it is directed towards experiment, use, technology itself; it is this which sets modern science apart from that of classical Greece, Babylon, or India. The contemporary production of scientific knowledge is, through the method of experiment, inherently committed to acting on the natural world in order to understand and control it. At the level of consciousness of individual scientists, a quite contrary view was commonly expressed from the nineteenth through to the mid-twentieth century. This emphasized the disinterested and nonutilitarian nature of the work of the man of science. Often quoted are the examples of the mathematician G. H. Hardy, who claimed that what he liked about mathematics was that it was no use to anyone, and of Ernest Rutherford, who, laying the foundations of nuclear physics at the Cavendish Laboratory, was to say that he saw no application for his work. Their belief that they were pursuing knowledge for knowledge's sake savors more of the social functions of premodern science, where science is on a par with other intellectual and aesthetic activities such as music or poetry, than of contemporary science. (The argument here is not that there is *no* science without a social function; it is that the dominant mode of production of scientific knowledge has social functions). In the case of Rutherford, the relevance of his pure science to military technology was to become all too clear despite his disclaimers. The significance of the Hardy-Weinberg equation for population genetics weakened, if less dramatically, Hardy's claim of uselessness. What is interesting, although we have not the space to explore it here, it how the unity of science and technology, the theory and practice of science, became institutionally and ideologically separated. What began as a technical division of labor between the development of theory and its application to particular practical problems became increasingly confused with a social division of labor. The distinction between "pure" science (and the word pure is not without its sociological connotations) and applied (impure, dirty?) science was and is sustained by the social institutions of science. The elite status of the "nonmanual" scientists as against the manual engineers has lingered on in a way that would satisfy Pythagoras himself.

It is perhaps worth reminding ourselves that this division of labor was neither considered necessary nor practised by the founding fathers of the Royal Society. As Robert Merton[5] points out, their researches ranged freely both over those questions that had a primarily theoretical interest and over those that were primarily practical. Robert Boyle was, for example, well aware of the connection between his discovery in 1662 that the volume of any gas varies inversely as the pressure at constant temperature, and problems of interior ballistics. For that matter, long before, Leonardo da Vinci had sought aristocratic patronage for his scientific research on the grounds that this would yield improved weaponry. So did Archimedes. However, what Merton points to is the way in which once the theoretical questions are posed, the development of theory takes on a life of its own, that is, that ideas become to some extent independent of the economic base. Hence, by the time of Britain's industrial revolution, theory and practice, in terms of scientific theory and industrial innovation, had become for the most part institutionally separated.

The Study of Science: Academic Internalism

To develop this argument about the contemporary unity of science and technology and their social functions, it is appropriate at this point to look back over the development of the history, philosophy, and sociology of science, and to try to demonstrate how it came to ignore the fundamentally Faustian nature of science. This is exemplified most clearly in the case of the sociologist, R. K. Merton, although we would argue that a similar case could be made within the history and philosophy of science. Much of Merton's early work, notably *Science Technology and Society in 17th century England,*[5] is best read as a continuing dialogue with the Marxist Boris Hessen[4] and his "externalist" view of the growth of science. Hessen's thesis was that Newtonian mechanics was developed in response to the needs of burgeoning capitalism. Merton, in exploring the influence of Puritanism in the development of seventeenth century science, stands to Hessen as Weber's Protestant Ethic juxtaposed with Marx's theory of the growth of capitalism. In this early period of his work, Merton is interested in the interpenetration of science in society and society in science. He did not eschew referring to the social forces that determine the direction of science, but did, in contradistinction to Hessen, attempt to show how science also develops autonomously, independent of social determinants. As his work developed, this opening, delicate probing of the internalist-externalist question moved increasingly towards internalism, paving the way for the development of "normal" sociology of science. The Mertonian paradigm thus became constituted as a variety of sociological internalism and, as is commonly the case, was a paradigm observed more rigidly by the subsequent followers than by the innovator. The paradigm is characterized by a preoccupation with science as a more or less autonomous subsystem. Essentially building on his work on the complex of values associated with Puritanism and the emergence of the Royal Society, Merton focused his interest on the scientific ethos itself. This preoccupation with the norms of science was encouraged by the notion of Michael Polanyi[21] of the scientific community as a self-governing collectivity. This variant of internalism ceased to address itself to questions of the interpenetration of science and the social order at the cognitive level, or even of scientists and the social order at the structural level. Instead, it interviewed Nobel Laureates, phage biologists, topologists, and high-energy physicists, and assumed that the activity of the whole scientific community, including industrial and defense scientists, could be interpreted through the study of the elite.

Thus the fundamental character of science and technology in their social functions was lost to sight.

In order to rediscover a sociology that takes into account scientific and technological policy, that is, the interpenetration of science and the state, we have to set aside the Mertonian paradigm, which emphasizes the self-governing and autonomous nature of science. It is not without irony that, at the very moment when the advent of war unequivocally destroyed the foundations of Polanyi's thesis, which was an effort to preserve science from the dreaded Marxist planners headed by J. D. Bernal, sociology was to conceive this curiously backward-looking conception of science. Polanyi's, and hence Merton's, community of self-governing scientists was to be destroyed in a real world which no longer asked *should* science be planned, but *how* should science be planned. In terms of social policy, this meant not *should* science serve the state, but *how* should science serve the state. During World War II even erstwhile *laissez-faire*-minded scientists energetically joined the "Bernalists" and the "Zuckermen" to plan science, mobilizing scientists to work on radar, bombing patterns, chemical-biological warfare, and of course, atomic weapons. The message was stamped home in the Manhattan Project, that uneasy alliance of J. Robert Oppenheimer and Major-General Groves, which was the embodiment of the most massive intervention of the state into science (and, for that matter, of scientists *vis-à-vis* the state) and yet took place within that most arcane of sciences, physics itself.

The Management of British Science

The change in the character of science of which the Manhattan Project marked the watershed, and which has led inexorably to its present managed status, so different from that to which the Mertonian paradigm addressed itself, may be seen at its clearest among capitalist nations. In Britain, the concern for tidy and unitary administrative structures often makes explicit what is hidden within the apparent multiplicity of agencies and the rhetoric of the scientific entrepreneur in the United States. The transition between *laissez-faire* and state-managed science is exemplified by the contrast between two seminal government reports on the relationship between state and science, separated by more than 50 years, years of which the Polanyi-Bernal debate and the Manhattan Project mark the midpoint. The two reports were those of Lord Haldane in 1918 and Lord Rothschild in 1972.

The Machinery of Government Report[22] was the culmination of a series of studies embarked upon by Haldane and his colleagues in the war years. It established the Research Council structure by which "pure" research has been funded in Britain ever since. The point for Haldane was very clear. A modern state needed science in order to survive—just how much was demonstrated in the early war years by the failures and limits of British technology against a Germany superior in chemistry, physics, and engineering. Haldane did not need the elaborate exercises of later policy-makers, such as the Department of Defense's *Project Hindsight,* to be confident of the links between basic science and defense and industry. Yet it was also apparent to him that these links were much mediated; to be effective, science and scientists needed space and protection from immediate production and military pressures. So the famous Haldane principle was enunciated by which the Councils were independent of the Departments of State which might be expected to be affected by this research (although such Departments were expected to conduct their own research as well). The advantage of this independence, as Haldane put it (para 67[a]) was as follows:

> It placed responsibility to Parliament (for the research) in the hands of a Minister who is in normal times free from any serious pressure of administrative duties, and is immune from any suspicion of being biased by administrative considerations against the application of the results of research.

Thus the "space" available for scientific autonomy was carefully defined and protected in the interests of efficiency, and the very space itself became hallowed as the cornerstone of scientific freedom until the end of the Second World War. From 1945 onwards, as we have argued elsewhere,[9] successive governments (whether Labour or Conservative) drew the net of state-science interaction tighter, until finally, under the 1970 Conservative government, the Rothschild report, *A Framework for Government Research and Development,*[23] challenged the Haldane principle head-on, and, over the vociferous protests of the scientific elite, was accepted as the future basis for the management of science.[24]

What Rothschild did was to state clearly that research and development were not autonomous, but had a purpose to be defined by the State and its industrial counterparts; policy decisions were not the free prerogative of scientists merely because they were scientists, except insofar as they also happened to hold other governmental or industrial positions (see below). Even the language of the Report was in a style which made the new relationship manifest; Hardy and Rutherford might turn in their graves.

> This report is based on the principle that applied r and d, that is, r and d with a practical application as its objective, must be done on a customer-contractor basis. The customer says what he wants, the contractor does it (if he can): and the customer pays.

Rothschild thereby makes more explicit than any of his counterparts in the United States the extent to which managed science has, under modern capitalism, become part of a managed society, whose management is itself scientifically founded. It is from this extension of scientific rationality, characteristic of the present phase of capitalism and state socialism, that the conception of science as first the domination of nature, and then the domination of man, has been born.

The Domination of Nature and the Domination of Man

The elision between knowledge and power, which had existed on a relatively *ad hoc* basis—close in time of war, neglected in peace—had thus by the mid-twentieth century become writ large and institutionalized. However, what had happened in this apparent fulfillment of the Baconian vision was that human progress, which was the underlying goal of the New Atlantis, became replaced by a technical progress. Thus, writing in the defense of Operation Plowshare, a proposal to use nuclear explosions to blast out deep harbors, the father of the American H bomb, Edward Teller, described science as progress that "cannot and will not be stopped."[25]

Where in the past the ideology of science proclaimed its socially liberatory function (much as official Soviet science still does, see below), Nagasaki and Hiroshima marked unequivocally what had only been glimpsed before—the alliance between the domination of nature by science and the domination of man by power.

Partly because the Bomb had been so devastating, scientists, as an elite, were unable to sustain the ideology that science and technology were socially progressive, yet they assumed that they carried particular political responsibilities in that they believed that the research they did, unlike that of the historian or artist, reacted very directly upon society. At the same time, there was the likelihood that the Bomb would be seen as an *inevitable* result of physics, so that anyone with qualms concerning its use would have to stop doing physics; the responsibility would have been too much (indeed many did go into biology for these reasons). The argument against this criticism was to claim the *neutrality* of science, declaring it to be a force either for good or evil depending upon the whims of society. It was merely the *application* of science that was nonneutral. This convenient conjuncture enabled many scientists in the two decades that followed to continue simultaneously to do "high" science, even accepting research grants from the military to do it, while at the same time professing radical political attitudes or arguing against particular developments in the arms race. Thus the discord between the objective reality of the uses of science and the consciousness of the scientist became almost complete.[26] The implications of the Bomb were seen as issues of the *abuse* of science, rather than as a social problem intrinsic to the character of science itself. This was the case whether the issues were raised in the liberal *Bulletin of the Atomic Scientists*, in the Marxist journal of the World Federation of Scientific Workers—*Scientific World*—or by the various groups of scientists active in the peace movement within the United States and Western Europe during the late 1940s and early '50s.

The critique of science as inherently geared to the domination of nature and thence of man, which had been developed by the neo-Marxist Frankfurt School of critical social theory, therefore remained initially virtually unheard, except by other social theorists. Unfettered by an allegiance to the particuar form of socialism emerging within the Soviet Union and subsequently within Eastern Europe, members of the Frankfurt School were able to continue the critical examination of the nature of alienation under increasingly corporate capitalism and bureaucratic socialism. Retaining their interest in the psychological dimensions of alienation, an interest elsewhere dismissed by orthodox Marxism as the concern of the early Marx, the Frankfurt School, and most notably Horkheimer,[27] Adorno,[28] Habermas,[29] and Marcuse,[30] was able to explore the ways in which the impersonal rationality of science extended into the political process itself.

The implication of this analysis is that, as it has developed under the conditions of industrialization in Western society, science has been concerned, not so much with ensuring that men and women live harmoniously with nature, but instead, first with the control and manipulation of nature, and then of one another.[31] This can be seen at many levels—from the choice of words used to express their activities by technological ideologues (the *conquest* of space, the *modification* of weather, the *exploitation* of natural resources, the *control* of brains and behavior) —to the recognition of all the unintended consequences of such technological advances ranging from the ecological hazards of dams to the drug-based medical practice of Britain or the USA. Where scientific and revolutionary optimists like Bernal had shared an inevitably progressive view of science (beautifully captured by Richard Gregory, the editor of *Nature* in the 1930s, who said "My grandfather preached the gospel of Christ, my father preached the gospel of socialism, I preach the gospel of science"), for the more pessimistic Frankfurt school it was not merely the *side effects* of technological production that were oppressive but the very nature of the technological product itself. Science and technology under these conditions could not but be oppressive. What is more, this oppression is reflected not merely in their products (the hardware of social control technology, from napalm and fragmentation weapons to Ritalin and psychosurgery), but also in the ideological role played by scientific theories in the preservation of the existing social order, from Social Darwinism in the nineteenth century to IQ testing or ethological theories of "innate" forms of human society today.[32]

This is clearly seen in Marcuse's *One Dimensional Man,* which portrays a social world pervaded by technological rationality. Marx had argued that the antagonism between nature and man, and hence man's alienation from nature, including his own nature, was integral to capitalist society. Science for Marx, and even more for Engels, still held something of an Enlightenment concept as harmonious to human progress.[33] In a century of the massive growth in the scale and power of science Marcuse discerns science and technology as a particular mode of rationality aiding human *pacification,* the contemporary and suffocating alternative to human liberation. Nor is it by chance that the struggles between *pacification* and *liberation* conceptualized by Marcuse find their echo in the real world struggles for national independence. Guerillas are part of national *liberation* movements; colonial and neocolonial powers, using all the armory of contemporary science and technology, speak of the *pacification* of the indigenous peoples.

Planning Science and Human Liberation

The contrasting views of science held by Marcuse, on the one hand, and Bernal, working in the classical Marxist tradition, on the other, might be tested in practice in terms of the experience of postrevolutionary societies like the Soviet Union and China. In the USSR the linking of science to social needs and the interests of state has been explicit and theory-based since 1917. Science, belonging to both the economic base and the superstructure, was to play a leading part in the achievement of human liberation, first through socialism and then through communism. In the early 1920s, during the period of N.E.P., it was considered sufficient to facilitate the work of the engineers and fund scientists on an increasing scale without exercising too close a control of either their ideology or products. Scientists themselves were divided, as Solomon[34] indicates in her study of conflict in rural Soviet sociology, between the bourgeois researchers trained in prerevolutionary Russia, and the young Marxists, who had been trained by them but who were working in and for the postrevolutionary society. As she makes clear, there was a sharp ideological and theoretical debate between them over the development of a theory of rural economic growth that would be harmonious with the needs of the developing Soviet socialist society. The debate was conducted by reasoned argumentation—by critique and countercritique. This style of conflict prevailed until Stalin imposed his own intellectual and cultural solution to this and many other areas of theoretical dispute.

The question opened in rural sociology, or even in the more notorious area of genetics, was not only concerned with the battle of ideas, between, for instance, the "bourgeois" paradigm of genetics, with its concept of fixed inheritance and chance mutations, and the "socialist" paradigm of infinite plasticity and environmental modification. It also concerned the class origins of the scientists themselves. The deep-bedded socialist view that knowledge is forged in practice favored Lysenko, the peasant and practical plant breeder (in this sense a cultural revolutionary), over the aristocratic geneticist Vavilov.[35]

Leaving aside the actual historical outcome, what we can see in the early phases of these struggles was the spontaneous attempt at a cultural revolution, but an attempt made *without* the clear theory of mass participation characteristic of Maoist thought. The attempt therefore became the victim of Stalin's administrative politics, whereby both "redness" and expertise were to be defined from the top. From the Great Break of 1927 onward[36] there was an attempt to link both the goals of technology and the ideology of the technologists themselves to the needs of communism, beginning with the engineers and spreading by the 1930s and 1940s to all branches of science.[37] Some of these scientists acted from solid philosophical conviction and others from terror; but both "camps"—the red and the expert—were themselves trapped in an increasingly bureaucratic and hierarchical society. In any event, for reasons discussed at greater length elsewhere,[26] the attempts, however motivated, to look for specifically proletarian forms of science have been modified in the last two decades into an assumption of the automatic elision between the needs of the Soviet state and the advances of neutral science.

It has been left to the Chinese revolution to advance the theory and practice of cultural revolution. Starting in 1951 from the Leninist perspective that "a scientist or engineer would come to accept communism through the data of his science and in his own way," Maoist theory had added the need for ideological remolding of intellectuals.[38] The Communist Party was faced with the double task of developing Chinese science and at the same time harnessing it to the needs of the people, particularly in production. The emphasis on production to be achieved through bureaucratic professionalism (Liu Shao Chi-ism) led to the perpetuation of hierarchy and the dominance of theory over practice. The cultural revolution, beginning in 1966, returned to the question of ideological remolding, but in a much more root-and-branch way, challenging bureaucracy and restoring the classical practice-theory-practice epistemology of Marxism, so that all forms of leadership that sought to derive their authority solely from expertise were heavily criticized. The extraordinary flowering and participative reorganization of many social institutions has been well documented for Western readers, particularly in medicine and to a lesser extent science. Horn[39] and others have discussed the changes in the biomedical sciences, reversing the normal drift to urban and hospital-based sophisticated technology beloved by medical technocrats, towards a rurally oriented system into which traditional medical methods otherwise "invalidated" by high technology have been reintegrated. Here, authority is based on service to the people expressed through expertise.[40] We know less from first-hand accounts of the workings-out and successes and failures of the scientific laboratories in the attempt to be both red and expert. Although there have been continuous attempts to proletarianize the laboratories, to make academic scientists learn from workers' experience, issues within science itself appear on the whole to have been dealt with by experiment and debate on the "hundred flowers" principle rather than by repeating the disaster of the Lysenko experience. The Stalinist solution to the problem of genetics was, from a very early period, considered by Mao and the Party to be an incorrect way of handling scientific questions. (It is perhaps worth noting here the CCP line on Stalin, who, while regarded as a great communist leader, is critizied in *The Question of Stalin* as having failed to distinguish contradictions among the people from those between the people. The former can be overcome; the latter must be exposed and fought).

Perhaps Suttmeier's distinction between Western "developmental science policy" and Chinese "integrative science policy" brings out the particular character of Chinese science.[41] As he observes, most research and development programs in the West, particularly in the 1950s and 1960s, were linked to specific problems approached within the framework of a reductionist cost-benefit analysis. Only now is it being painfully learned in the West that a more systemic approach, which stresses the interaction of, for example, environmental or transportation issues, is necessary. Such an integrative approach, in a much wider and deeper sense, has been fundamental to the Chinese analysis.

By contrast, in orthodox Soviet Writings today, such as the essays by Mikhail Millionshchikov (vice-president of the USSR Academy of Sciences) and others in *The Scientific and Technological Revolution*,[42] science and technology are seen as value-free (i.e., there is no specifically *socialist* biology, and the explosive debates of the Lysenko period are dismissed as misguided). The maximization of their potential for human welfare can only take place within the framework of the Soviet system. It is taken for granted, therefore, that under Soviet socialism state and science are in intimate correspondence by way of an elaborate policy-making machinery, and indeed, that bureaucratic professionalism is an efficient and desirable way to perpetuate this correspondence (see, for example, Kapitsa on the question of how the scientific elite should be recruited[43]). However, in order to maintain *both* that science is value-free and that it corresponds to the needs of the people in a beneficient Soviet society, it is necessary to argue that in capitalist societies, state and science are in contradiction. As Millionshchikov puts it "the principle of private enterprise in the age of nuclear energy, electronics and cybernetics will become increasingly exposed as historically obsolete." Scientific rationality, without being made over to a specifically socialist science, is thus supposed to expose the irrationality of capitalism. It is not necessary to be Marcuse, or for that matter to work in Solzhenitzyn's *First Circle,* to see the falsity of such a proposition.

Scientific Factory or Scientific Community?

This is not to argue a naive convergence theory, for the economic base of the Soviet state socialist system is quite different from that of Western capitalism, but in both societies there has been a bringing of the needs of science into close correspondence with those of state and industry. In this sense, the criticism of science as oppressive and dominating nature may also be generalized, for it describes the situation in both societies. In addition, the changed mode of production of scientific knowledge has resulted in a shift in the internal social structure of science.

Seen most conspicuously in "big science," where a whole laboratory may sign one short paper, this change has been widely recognized as the shift from craft production to the industrial production of knowledge.[15, 44] Where scientists once worked as individual "producers" of knowledge, now they work in large, hierarchically organized teams characterized by an increasingly refined division of labor. Each scientist, or more accurately, each scientific worker, for so the rank and file of the scientific factories of today must be termed, has fragmented, partial skills, and is bound to a purpose only fully understood by the project director and those who set the goals of the group or the laboratory. This fragmentation of scientific work and knowledge began, as André Gorz[45] points out, in Germany in the chemistry industry some ninety years ago when Carl Duisberg of Bayer organized and divided the tasks of the chemists.

The process has continued and expanded, science by science, through physics to molecular biology. Scientific workers become like factory workers, defined by the machine they tend, so that we have lathe operators and nuclear magnetic resonance (nmr) operators, typists and computer programmers, n.c. machine operators and spectroscopists.

The significance of this change cannot be overrated. Where in the nineteenth century Whewell recognized the gentlemanly nature of the pursuit of knowledge in his phrase "cultivators of science," professionalism was marked by the term "scientist." Now with the industrialization of science a proletariat has emerged, the rank and file scientific workers. Scientific workers in industrial and governmental research establishments have been found to be indifferent to the norms of science and instead are preoccupied by conditions of work, pay, security, and prospects.[46] The earlier commitment to "public knowledge,"[47] where the reward was obtained by acclaim by peers, eponymity, or prizes, is today irrelevant in most of the research system.

We cannot explore here in any detail the political and trade union responses of the scientific workers both to the situation whereby the scientific community has become the scientific factory and to the deepening economic crisis of capitalism.[26, 32] We can only refer to the considerable growth in scientific trade unions, which is likely to extend further as the threat of unemployment grows. Perhaps even more significant than the growth of the unions' political interest in science has been a general move toward radicalization among scientific workers and students, catalyzed by consciousness of the role of science and technology in the Indochina War; and a profound questioning of the whole social role and structure of science and its institutions, and indeed of the epistemological base of science itself. Indeed experience of the practice and theory of organizations like SESPA (Scientists and Engineers for Social and Political Action) in the United States and BSSRS (British Society for Social Responsibility in Science) in Britain is reflected throughout the analysis presented in this paper.

Despite, or perhaps because of, this transition from scientific community to scientific factory, there remains, leading, planning and administering science, a scientific elite who are happy to share and perpetuate the myth of the self-governing community of scientists. It is only these, as we have said, who have been "visible" so far as much of the academic sociology, philosophy, and history of science are concerned. It is only these whom Shils, contrasting scientists with the "laity," urges to keep faith[48] and who share in Monod's conception of science as humanity's noblest activity.[49] It is arguable that sociologically only this group can legitimately be termed scientists. The relative smallness of the elite group is worth emphasizing, especially in the context of the conduct of science and technology decision-making. In the United States, for example, it has been estimated that some 200–300 key decision-makers, primarily scientists, constitute the inner elite out of a total scientific work force of some two million. For the rank and file scientific workers, alienation is the norm.

Disenchantment or Hope?

The thesis of this paper expresses an analysis that is increasingly shared by social theorists, both radical and liberal in persuasion. The view of the interpenetration of science and society is one of increasing disenchantment. Together, the domination of nature and bureaucratic rationality are seen by many to represent an almost irreversible and potentially disastrous trend. Historically, under conditions of extreme crisis, liberal social theorists look to individuals for solutions—whether within one institution, in this case science, or at the whole societal level. Yet because of the experience during this century of heroic individuals, of charismatic figures, this solution is as daunting as the problem.

The stoic pessimism of contemporary liberal theory also stems from a limited perspective of alternative social forms. Their comparisons are confined to those between capitalist countries and the USSR, without recognizing that while there are important differences in economic organization between the USA and the USSR, at a cultural level there are many continuities. Unless the cultural alternatives, such as those aborted in the Soviet Union but continuing to be explored by the Chinese, are taken into account, the prognosis for scientific and technical policy and society itself can only be gloomy.

References

1. BOWDEN, LORD. 1965. Expectations for science: to the limits of growth. New Scientist **27**: 849.
2. BISHOP, A. R. 1968. Nature **219**: 15.
3. HANDLER, P. Address to the Biochemical Society, London. December 1969.
4. HESSEN, B. 1931. The social and economic roots of Newton's *Principia*. *In* Science at the Cross Roads. N. Bukharin et al., Ed. Kniga. London, England. (Reprinted 1973. Cass. London.)
5. MERTON, R. K. 1938. Science, Technology and Society in 17th Century England. St. Catherine Press. Belgium. (Reprinted 1970. Fertig. New York, N.Y.)
6. NEEDHAM, J. 1954. Science and Civilization in China. University Press. Cambridge, England.
7. NEEDHAM, J. 1964. Science and society in East and West. *In* The Science of Science. Goldsmith, M. and A. Mackay, Eds. Souvenir Press. London, England.
8. BERNAL, J. D. 1939. The Social Function of Science. Routledge. London, England.
9. ROSE, H. & S. ROSE. 1969. Science and Society. Allen Lane. London, England.
10. PRICE, D. K. 1954. Government and Science. Oxford University Press. New York, N.Y.
11. GILPIN, R. 1962. Atomic Scientists and Nuclear Weapons Policy. Princeton University Press. Princeton, N.J.
12. BARBER, R. 1966. The Politics of Research. Public Affairs Press. Washington, D.C.
13. SCHOOLER, D. 1971. Science, Scientists and Public Policy. Free Press. New York, N.Y.
14. GREENBERG, D. 1969. The Politics of Pure Science. Penguin. Harmondsworth, England.
15. SALOMON, J. J. 1973. Politics and Science. Macmillan. London, England.
16. CARTER, C. F. & B. R. WILLIAMS. 1957. Industry and technical progress. Oxford University Press. London, England.

17. Science Policy Research Unit. 1974. Annual report, Sussex University Press, Falmer.
18. WEINBERG, A. 1963. Criteria for scientific choice. Minerva 1: 2.
19. LEVY-LEBLOND, J. M. & A. JAUBERT. 1973. Critique et Autocritique de la Science. De Seuil. Paris, France.
20. BLUME, S. 1974. Toward a Political Sociology of Science. Collier-Macmillan. London, England.
21. POLANYI, M. 1945. The Logic of Liberty. Routledge. London.
22. Haldane Report. 1918. Machinery of Government Report. His Majesty's Stationary Office. London, England.
23. Rothschild Report. 1972. A Framework for Government Research and Development. Her Majesty's Stationary Office. London, England.
24. WILLIAMS, R. 1973. Some political aspects of the Rothschild affair. Sci. Stud. 3: 31–46.
25. TELLER, E. 1970. Can a progressive be a conservationist? New Scientist 45: 346–8.
26. ROSE, H. & S. ROSE. 1972. The radicalisation of science. In The Socialist Register. R. Miliband and J. Saville, Eds. Merlin Press. London, England.
27. HORKHEIMER, M. 1947. Eclipse of Reason. New York, N.Y.
28. ADORNO, T. W. & M. HORKHEIMER. 1947. Dialektik der Aufklarung. Amsterdam, The Netherlands.
29. HABERMAS, J. 1971. Toward a Rational Society. Heinemann. London, England.
30. MARCUSE, H. 1964. One Dimensional Man: Studies in the Ideology of Advanced Industrial Society. Boston, Mass.
31. LEISS, W. 1972. The Domination of Nature. Braziller. New York, N.Y.
32. ROSE, H. & S. ROSE. Ideology in/of the Natural Sciences. Penguin. Harmondsworth, England. In press.
33. SCHMIDT, A. 1971. The Concept of Nature in Marx. New Left Books. London, England.
34. SOLOMON, S. G. 1973. Controversy in social science: Soviet rural studies in the 1920s. Ph.D. thesis, Columbia University, New York, N.Y.
35. LEWONTIN, R. & R. LEVINS. Political aspects of the Lysenko affair. In Ideology in/of the Natural Sciences. H. Rose & S. Rose, Eds. In press.
36. JORAVSKY, D. 1961. Soviet Marxism and Natural Science. Routledge & Kegan Paul. London, England.
37. GRAHAM, L. 1972. Science and Philosophy in the Soviet Union. Knopf. New York, N.Y.
38. SUTTMEIER, R. 1970. Party views of science: The record from the first decade. China Quart. (Oct.–Dec.)
39. HORN, J. S. 1969. Away with all Pests. Paul Hamlyn. London, England.
40. NEEDHAM, J., J. ROBINSON & T. RAPER. 1971. Hand and Brain in China. Anglo-Chinese Education Institute.
41. SUTTMEIER, R. Thinking about science policy: A Chinese comparison. Paper given at the International Sociological Association Meeting, Toronto, Ontario, Canada, 1974.
42. MILLIONSHCHIKOV, H. 1972. In The Scientific and Technological Revolution: Social Effects and Prospects.: 13–28. Progress Publishers. Moscow, USSR.
43. KAPITSA, P. 1973. Basic factors in the organisation of science and how they are handled in the USSR. Daedalus 102 (2): 167–176.
44. RAVETZ, J. 1971. Scientific Knowledge and Its Social Problems. Oxford University Press. London, England.
45. GORZ, A. The class character of science and scientists. In Ideology in/of the Natural Sciences. H. Rose and S. Rose, Eds. In press.
46. ELLIS, N. The scientific worker. Ph.D. thesis, University of Leeds, 1969.
47. ZIMAN, J. 1968. Public Knowledge. Cambridge University Press. Cambridge, England.
48. SHILS, E. 1974. Faith, utility and the legitimacy of science. Daedalus 103 (3): 1–16.
49. MONOD, P. 1972. Chance and Necessity. Cape. London, England.

DISCUSSION

UNIDENTIFIED SPEAKER: I am dismayed that only about 20 percent of the scientists in a given field are aware and knowledgeable about science and public policy, both in this country and internationally. Isn't it true of all fields that only about

10 or 20 percent are interested in the problems and that the other 80 or 90 percent are interested in making a living and succeeding in their given field? Does that annoy the science philosophers?

DR. S. ROSE: One part of the thesis of our paper is that the bulk of scientific workers in this society are alienated labor. That is, they're doing a job and their relationship with the work that they do is, in many respects, closer to the relationship of other workers producing material goods. The correct political analysis says that the response in this particular sort of situation should and is likely to be one which goes through collective action and through the development of scientific unions of the sort that we were talking about.

It's not altogether surprising, therefore, to find that most scientific workers are concerned with bread and butter issues. Why shouldn't they be? These are among the most important issues that they have to face. It's the privileged and the elite who can afford to speculate, often without adequate analysis, about the ethical issues which are raised when people talk about social responsibility and science.

What is much more important and optimistic is to view the growth of scientific unionization and of radicalization among science students as the demonstration of an attempt to come to grips with the very real nature of the relationship of science to state and society and to find effective political means of acting upon it.

DR. I. R. LAPIDUS (*Stevens Institute of Technology, Hoboken, N. J.*): I noticed, Dr. Rose, that in your presentation you tended to confuse words like science and technology, referring to engineers versus scientists, and scientific workers versus scientists when they are not the same thing at all. For example, in a given laboratory in "big science," as you call it, there may be one or two scientists in a group of twenty or thirty people. And to lump all these people into one group and to discuss alienation of the worker in that context without taking into account the differing natures of the work being done by the various people is to confuse the issue.

You alluded to the fact that modern science today is in a position similar to that of the high-energy physicists in England who have to decide whether or not they're going to join CERN. It is true throughout science that science can't be done cheaply anymore. Therefore you have to have a benefactor, and for the most part that benefactor is the government. One of the problems that science is facing today in its relationship with society and government is that it is impossible to do science without the support of the government. What bothered me about your analysis of this was that I had the feeling that you were looking at a collection of ants who are just being moved along by some natural forces, rather than realizing that a man like the President can make a decision on a Tuesday morning which can have billion-dollar effects, and that these things happened precipitously in the past few years and did not represent a gradual evolution of society. These were hard decisions made by a few people in the White House and they created massive catastrophies in the scientific community in a very short period of time. They're not strictly sociological-type occurrences, but rather hard political decisions. If you fail to recognize this, you really miss a lot of what's happened in American science, at least. I'm not familiar with what's going on in Great Britain.

Again, I think it's important to make the distinction between people who are scientists *as* scientists and people who simply work as part of the scientific process. A person who comes in as a technician in the morning and routinely carries through some operations which in practice are very similar to those of a die-punch operator in a factory is not a scientist, even though he may have a bachelor's degree in some kind of science. He is not functioning as a scientist. Therefore, to include these people in the scientific community as such disturbs the statistics enough that you might not get a handle on the real story of the relationship between science and society.

DR. H. ROSE: I certainly agree with this, but you think there's a bigger scientific community than I do. It is true that there are more and more technicians, to use your language, and fewer and fewer scientists. Because science, as it has grown into an absolutely massive activity, has a limited number of generals and rather a large number of foot soldiers, and only the generals are scientists. The rest are, to use my language, scientific workers; to use your language, technicians. However, they're not called technicians—they're still called scientists. And a lot of them are told that underneath their arm and their test tube, they carry the field marshall's baton. And it's a lie. They don't. They're never going to get to the top. For example, how do you get your Nobel prize? Not by being a "good scientist," but by working in a laboratory where there's a Nobel Laureate. It's only in a particular milieu in which it is possible to do certain things. So we're talking about a world that is much more like industry than science is willing to admit. After all, it's had to ask a man who thinks of himself as a scientist to acknowledge that he is actually only a cog in a machine that is run by others. However, reality has a way of coming in, particularly at times of economic crisis, when it's no longer possible to deal in myths, and when you have to get down to the hard business of earning a living. It seems to me that at that moment we all start to agree on terms.

As a sociologist I always regard social statistics—which are usually put together by government bodies—as mainly revealing of the values that went into the setting-up of the categories that produced the statistics. They don't tell you much else.

On the question of science and technology, which is where you began, I simply disagree with you. I believe that science and technology are one, and that the convenient distinction that we make for day to day operational purposes has no meaning in terms of the nature of modern science because the two interlock. The particular character of modern science is that science and technology are indivisible.

We do agree on your last point concerning science and state support. Scientists who talk a line about neutrality and the independence of science have actually sat rather resolutely on the Jason committees and the like and have, in fact, shown that in order to get their money, they will work extremely closely with the state. The situation is rather like that of nineteenth century economics and the invisible hand of the market. That is, scientists see that the interests of the state are peculiarly the interests of science. And equally the state sees that science's needs are the needs of the state. And, of course, it is very true, because science actually produces material wealth, and massive military technology, and has always done so. The state and science sit very close together. What is particularly interesting to me, speaking as a sociologist, is how people ever thought that science was autonomous, that it was separate from the state, because it has always needed resources, whether they were the kind provided by a leisured class, such as those Haldane used to have his own laboratory in his big room in Oxford, or whatever. And Haldane's case was the exception. Whether it was Leonardo da Vinci chumming up with a particular prince, saying you give me resources and I'll make you ballistic weaponry; or Archimedes, or whoever, it can be seen that science has always had more than one footsie under the state's table. And quite frequently, in historical terms the state has been far from benign to great masses of people; indeed it seems to me that the modern state is far from benign. The example of the complicity of scientists and the state was evident in the prosecution of the Indochina War, where science and technology were so deeply linked. Dr. Langer said these ways were abstract; but to me they seem quite concrete. Witness the assembling of the most arcane scientists, physicists, to develop the most concrete and horrible technological forms. I fail to understand how you can separate science and technology conceptually, practically, institutionally, or in terms of the people themselves.

DR. S. ROSE: Dr. Lapidus, I just want to pick up on one other point that you made, in which you implied that the decisions made by one man sitting in power would, in fact, be the way in which massive social changes were brought about, that one man could make a decision that might result in unemployment or would waste billions of dollars or set into motion massive expenditures on science and technology.

Now, I don't really think that this mode of analysis is adequate. At one level you can explore the way in which decisions are made in terms of one man doing X (and as Hilary would say, it is generally one man, rather than one woman, doing X). This sort of analysis is not very helpful because it doesn't actually let one understand why it is that particular individuals are the way they are in a particular social context, or why, in the broader social context, particular decisions are made. It would be hard to argue that the Indochina War and the development of science and technology associated with it were the decisions of one man. It would be easy to analyze in terms of the social-psychological motivations or stresses in the White House, but this would not actually help one to understand the broader social forces, the things that drive science and technology forward, the broad sweep that makes, for example, unemployment among engineers, which was a particularly acute problem towards the end of the 1960's, in particular the period between 1968 and 1972. These occurrences cannot be related very usefully to the activities of one or even a few men; they are much better understood and analyzed in terms of much broader social history. It's not that one man is irrelevant; it's just that you're ignoring the pressures and events that actually make that person do what he does at that particular time or put that particular person there. To make a distinction between what one man does and the social structure that actually moves that man into that position is to make an artificial distinction and one which doesn't help; it mystifies, because it means that everything occurs at random. You get a psychopath and you get the Indochina War; you get a nonpsychopath and you get a space program: That is not really a useful way to understand such complex events.

DR. FEIGELSON: I share Dr. Lapidus's discomfort with the kinds of conclusions your analysis led you to. Of course there is an important element of applied consequences to science, and surely there are lots of people in government who would share exactly your analysis and who view the pragmatic consequences of science as the end of science. Fortunately, this opinion is not universal, even on the part of government officials. I think there may be a greater appreciation, even in the minds of powerful people in decision-making positions, as to the cultural role of science than you seem to acknowledge. I think it is necessary to recognize the fundamental nature of science as a cultural enterprise of man and to recognize that it has certain similarities to poetry, music, etc.; it is necessary to acknowledge that the accumulation of knowledge of this sort by certain techniques that are formalized under the title of science is a creation of the human intellect. To just deal with the pragmatic consequences of science is to grossly distort it. If, for example, you had the experience of sitting on committees where research grant applications are screened and reviewed, and if you saw that only a certain fraction of these projects can be funded, and if you participated in the kinds of review and heard the kinds of discussions as to the criteria applied in judging which of these applications should be funded, then I suspect that your views would be modified because the criteria are considerably more esoteric and less pragmatic than you seem to feel.

UNIDENTIFIED SPEAKER: I'm speaking from a measure of enthusiasm, but also from a measure of ignorance. I believe I remember correctly a quotation from another Englishman, Chesterton, who said that "Christianity hasn't failed; it just hasn't been tried." I'm not trying to defend that particular theory, but I think that the theory that is essentially being written off by you is the concept of any input of individual creativity, individual reality, apart from an essentially externally determined reality. However, there are some laws every bit as abstruse as the idea that there is someone out there sending us communications on golden tablets or little red books. Perhaps the fault in your analysis is the idea that these things must necessarily be governed by some sort of greater force. My own prejudice is that these external forces exert less influence in human affairs than either the classical religionist or the modern Marxist believes.

DR. H. ROSE: The concept of science as culture simply in that dimension wasn't the concern of the paper. What we were trying to talk about is how science as culture has changed from being something that could be regarded as progressive in its social form and in itself elegant, beautiful, and exciting. We are asking you to put to one side the question of the aesthetic considerations and to look at the social function of science. And we must recognize that this social function has changed and is not progressive. Now this statement is by no means something that comes out of a little red book. Major conservative theorists like Jacques Ellul make precisely the same indictment of science. At the very moment that we feel ourselves to be neither on the left or on the right we should start thinking, because at that moment we are actually in the middle. If we look back to that moment of crisis in the nineteenth century when capitalism emerged, considerations of the social theorists of the right and of those on the left were the same. That is: they were obsessed by the horror of a capitalist society in which human beings were alienated from each other. The conservatives and the Marxists were talking about the same thing. The formation of capitalism created a tremendous human crisis. Conservatives talked about the community and the village and the mine shaft, while Marx talked about solidarity and warmth. But both were looking for the same things—certain human and philosophical considerations—which were lost in capitalism.

The crisis that is hitting this particular culture at this particular time is a massive one having to do with how we live. What we've got now is the scientific culture oppressing people. Jacques Ellul has said, "Psychology begins by wanting to understand man and ends by manipulating him." The same may be said of science, and we must heed the warning implied. It doesn't do any good to go off and say: we don't have to listen to that 'cause it's red talk or Right talk. We have to attend to what is happening here and now with the scientific culture. We are in too serious a situation to start labeling discussion as coming out of a red book or out of a black book or out of any other book. We've got to come to grips with the issue of the scientific culture. It's deadly serious, and we can't afford to label.

PHILIP SIEKEVITZ: I was interested in your implication of the "schizophrenic" attitude that many of us scientists have. I feel, and I think most scientists realize deep down, that we are "looking for crumbs" in our work. We like to do our own research and our own thing, but we really can't. We devise "mischievous" ways by which we can do this. There is a huge amount of money in this country for cancer research. Well, we devise ways to use this money in our own way; we don't believe what the advisors or the directors say. We're really looking for one hundred dollars out of one million dollars.

I would like to offer a few of the historical reasons for this "schizophrenia" of science. Originally, this attitude was raised as a sort of philosophical stance against that of a Church-dominated society. In order to gain independence, the scientists of that time set up a whole theory of neutrality. They had no value systems at all because if they acknowledged any value system, they would be very quickly suppressed by the dominant religious value system of the time. So they manufactured a theory, and I use the word "manufactured" quite seriously, of a neutral science, which had no value systems from above in philosophy or theory. Consequently, this idea of value-free science has been passed on through the writings of scientific theorists and apologists. So we're in a situation where many of us, at present, go back to this seventeenth or eighteenth century idea of scientific neutrality. But during these past two centuries the importance of science and technology has grown to be so overwhelming that the rulers of society in every culture have seen to it that the scientists have to be a part of the social structure. So, what has happened right now is that we have an outmoded theory of the neutrality of science, which was formulated about two centuries ago, which is in conflict with the reality of today. I believe that many of us in the laboratory are aware of this and as a result straddle the fence, trying to do our best to serve our own individual ideas about what science should be and what it means to us, and meanwhile serving the state as well.

When I started out in science about twenty-five years ago, it was relatively easy to get some money to work on whatever you wanted. But in the last few years, some of my graduate students or postdoctoral fellows are getting jobs where they're actually told what they have to do. There isn't much of a chance for these young people now to go out on their own, except for a very small segment of exceptional students. And in these last twenty-five years there has been the realization of what the atom bomb means and the realization of the implications of scientific research for technology for the country. We are in a crisis situation in science, but I think scientists realize this. We're doing our best and fighting it in our own individual ways by being sort of subversive of the order. It's the only way we, as scientists, can survive. It's the only way, for example, that artists can survive.

DR. S. ROSE: I agree with a great deal of what Dr. Siekevitz said: in a sense, the watershed is there. I also want to address this question of science as culture. I'm very well aware that a large number of us rip off cancer grants or whatever in order to do things that we think are more interesting. And there's always the argument then about whether, in fact, this rip-off is serving us better than it's serving them; or serving truth better than it's serving them, or however it might be. It's a delicate balance. And those of us who serve on grant-reviewing committees see this coming up again and again; it's not an infrequent phenomenon.

We are not trying to propound a monolithic argument that says that science is so tightly controlled by the system at the moment that there is no space. If that were so, it would indeed be a very gloomy prospect. The one thing that we do know about our society, and about humanity within it, is that we are not operating under an iron law of history which is external to man, and that we are pawns within that system. No serious revolutionary theorist would ever maintain such a thing, because the important thing about human beings is their capacity to create themselves and to transform the society in which they live. In that sense, science has a real and very positive role to play. The picture that we would put forward is not wholly and totally gloomy. For one thing, it works, even if crudely. Rockets do go to the moon, and penicillin does kill some organisms in some circumstances. Science is about the real world out there.

Now, the point about science and the world is our *understanding* of it. The science we do is continuously being reflected through the mirrors of us as individuals operating in a social context. And so there is the ideology within science which obscures the real world out there, and those pictures of it that are moving forward towards something better.

Now, the point about our present situation is that the vast bulk of the scientific machinery has been co-opted for particular purposes: the manipulation of man, the domination of nature, and the maintenance of the social structure and the social order. Those of us doing what we might regard as the most pure and esoteric science on one level must recognize that another level exists, which is about science as culture and the way the real world is. Both levels reflect the presuppositions we have about the sort of society in which we live, and the sorts of paradigms we have of the world reflect this. And this in itself prevents us from understanding the real world out there. Also, what we do is susceptible to being used in ways that aren't rip-offs for us, but are ways of insuring that society or the state goes on manipulating and controlling the masses of the people within it. This constant tension within the structure of science is what makes it at the same time an oppressive and a dominating force, and at the same time potentially subversive and potentially capable of being utilized for the re-creation and for the positive development of man.

Most of the contemporary criticism of science derives from the fact that the dominating aspect of science has been in the ascendancy over the last two decades. I don't want to use these very crude dualistic forms to discuss this problem, because I think the interactions are much more complex than that, but for the moment, let's recognize that this negative aspect is in fact so important and so overwhelming that the whole practice and structure of science has become dominated by it.

Here it is no longer possible to plead a cultural argument. Science is a cultural force which also produces plastic fragmentation weapons and electronic battlefields and psychosurgery. Under these circumstances, one has very carefully to analyze the forces involved. To retreat from this analysis into the cultural argument or into saying "that's not science; that's technology and doesn't count," is to chicken out of what is the major part of the intellectual task that faces us today.

SEYMOUR MELMAN: I would wish to attach a responsibility to all formulators of socially determined systems, and that is to specify the limits of that determinism. Unless these limits are specified, then an inescapable implication of contemplating a determined social process is the prospect of seeing oneself as without possibility of acting in any willful way to alter its direction or effect.

The paper just presented by the Roses had the quality of formulating a determined system. It did not indicate at any point any crucial limits to that determinism. I wish to suggest two such possible limits. One is: in every decision process there is no decision simply by the issuance of an instruction. It also requires willing acceptance and willing implementation. So one limit on any decision process—even in the most highly structured, managerial and hierarchical situation, including that of state bureaucracies—is the willingness of the participants to receive and to implement. Where that willingness is absent, the system starts cracking, and decision-makers cease to be decision-makers. We've seen a number of relatively small, but nevertheless quite important examples of that process in the United States during the last few years.

A second aspect of this first limit is the willingness of scientists to accept the societal and occupational values of the decision-makers in the system. If these values seem old-fashioned and to come from an era of individual initiative and enterprise and achievement in science, that doesn't take away from their quality of being values. A central issue implied by the Roses is the issue of what alternative values might scientists entertain and attempt to implement with respect to their work.

The second limiting point: who shall decide about work in science? Shall it be decided by bureaucrats, managers, boards, committees, however designated; or should it be decided by scientists themselves? If the latter is to be contemplated, then by what conceivable decision processes, by what modes of social organization might this be done?

I won't press the matter further except to underscore that a critique of the present managerialism and growth of state bureaucracy in the major industrial states is, of itself, very often effective in arguing the power, inevitability, irreversibility, and Golem-like qualities of this system, and the helplessness of all individuals involved. The only exit from that effect is the attempt to formulate alternatives in the decision process even if we are unable to forecast the success of a particular effort to anticipate the long-term historical development. All actions that hand the decision process over science to those who do the work in science reverse the policy of alienated and managerial control over science. The modes of action and organization that will effect such a reversal are to be welcomed.

DR FEIGELSON: Part of our problem is semantic, because if you do not distinguish the body of knowledge and the way scientists function and the body of knowledge that they generate from the applications of this knowledge, you will not have words that will allow you to distinguish the person studying microbial sensitivity to various agents in an attempt to cure a disease from the person studying the same thing in order to wage bacterial warfare. If we insist on calling all of this by the same word, we will not be able properly to analyze the situation. A distinction must be made between scientific procedures and scientific knowledge and the directions to which they are applied, which working scientists call technology. Knowledge can be used for good or bad purposes, depending upon one's value judgments. Tools can be used both to build and to destroy; the tools themselves are not evil. If you continue to fail to distinguish between science and technology, discussion will become very difficult.

ELIZABETH BARRETT: I'd like to consider medicine apart from the rest of the sciences because this is an area in which we still have contact with the individual person or the relative of the person receiving medical treatment. Thus the recipient of the treatment at least has an opportunity to see how the medical scientist applies the tools that he has, which is not the case in other scientific fields such as warfare technology, environmental control, or communications.

CHARLES HALPERN: I'm a lawyer involved in various efforts to impose some social control over the process of science and technology. I have often had a feeling that even the most benign developments must, in the context of America today, be greeted with mixed feelings or even terror. We have mentioned the subject of psychosurgery and other techniques for controlling human behavior. My involvement with psychosurgery over the past couple of years has led me to the position that any new understandings that we've gained about the mechanisms of the brain are extremely dangerous. A friend of mine, a neurosurgeon in Washington, told me about a marvelous new machine that they have at Georgetown Medical School that permitted great insights into brain process and would permit early diagnosis of stroke and various other intercranial phenomena. He was very excited about its therapeutic potential, but what it suggested to me was also the likelihood that this new knowledge of the brain would be abused in hastening the next round of psychosurgery.

UNIDENTIFIED SPEAKER: Two days ago the *New York Times* reported a story which at first doesn't seem to bear much relevance to what we are now discussing. It was reported that the City of New York subsidizes the arts in the city to the tune of millions of dollars a year. And you wonder: What does the city get out of it? I think that it's a kind of bribe to the people of New York to their well-being; a bribe from the people to themselves. And that's the way we scientists are operating. The government is giving us a bribe. They're letting us use some of their money. We all realize that most of the scientific money is used for technology. We all realize that there is no difference between science and technology. Whatever we do in the laboratory today could be technology tomorrow. They let us do something we might want to do because they need us.

I want to tell another story about the culture. About two or three years ago, at the annual meeting of the American Society of Biological Chemists, the question came up of what can we do to get more money from the government. The people in attendance at this meeting were involved with the Society and with the National Academy of Sciences, and the present head of the National Academy was there. I got up and said: Why can't we go to Congress and tell them to subsidize some science because it's a cultural activity just like education. We give money to education, we give to the arts, so why not give to science? And I was laughed down. Why? Because everybody knew that this is not why the government gives money to scientists.

DR. I. R. LAPIDUS: I don't want to belabor the points I made before, but I don't feel my remark was adequately responded to: When an example of something is given it is inadequate to refute it by saying that it's never always that way.

Before the conference ends it may be useful to discuss the distinction between social forces that are going to determine the relationship between science and society and the actual policy decisions that can be made in a short period of time. To deal with massive social forces as a group of scientists may be very difficult. On the other hand, for those decisions made by the President in the Oval Office on any given day it would be advantageous to have a science adviser there to tell him: don't do that today. There we can make an impact. I don't believe that we, as scientists, in the short run can change the intellectual climate of the country nor can we change the nature of the congressional appropriation. But we can exert a certain amount of influence on decisions as to allocation of money. To the extent that we can be influential, it will be on a person-to-person basis, and will be a reflection of the belief expressed at this meeting that scientists are people and not just elements of some sociological group.

DR. LANGER: The time has come for the Roses to respond to the many comments that have been made. Many of the points taken up here will undoubtedly come up again in the next two days. At least we now have been provided with a base from which to consider the range of possibilities for the achievement of a science that really does something to improve the quality of life.

DR. H. ROSE: There are two briefs that we've got here. One is the brief for the meeting, which all of us share in some respect. Then there is our particular brief, which is to examine questions of political philosophy. Obviously, this isn't going to give us quick answers to questions of tactics, for our discussion has been more concerned with strategy.

We certainly agree with Seymour Melman's point about the need to specify the limits of determinism. That was why we used the example of China as an alternative society. As a society that is trying to work things out differently, China must be viewed as a kind of enormous laboratory. The other alternative is to take Dr. Siekevitz's position, which is what we call "stoic liberalism," where the scientist acts individually, trying not to let anything terrible happen with the science he is working on. Look at what happened to Galston: he worked on plant hormones, only to discover that his work was being used to make defoliants for Indochina. Now, what you try to do is to make sure that the "blighters" don't get it, and keep your science in a reasonably good direction. And that may be the way we have to live day by day. But overall, we cannot ignore the strategic questions. We have got to look very seriously at big alternative societies, and big alternative experiments.

A really critical question was raised: Who shall decide? I would, of course, want to include more than just scientists. The British Health Service has been run by the doctors for long enough, and it's fairly awful. Professional syndicalism is no substitute for democracy. Power has got to be taken out of the hands of the few, and given to the many.

As to the question of the separation of knowledge and the application of that knowledge, Charles Halpern answered that very concretely, showing how the generation of basic knowledge and the resulting technology have a very tight relationship today. Analytically they can be separated, but they have a nasty way of jumping together again. Try and split the difference between technology and science in, as it were, a high-energy accelerator laboratory. Maybe medieval theologians can handle the question of separation, but I can't.

When Elizabeth Barrett spoke of medicine, she was talking of the human side of the potential problems Charles Halpern was pointing to. In certain areas, such as biology, the new knowledge and the new technologies get very close and are very powerful, particularly with respect to such issues as psychosurgery, the use of Ritalin, and the so-called I.Q. debate. It is in these kinds of areas that the knowledge base and the technology are tied up. If you didn't have a theory of knowledge about genetic theory of human intelligence, and you didn't have an I.Q. testing kit, you couldn't produce some of the social nonsense of categorizing people in such crude ways as clever, medium clever, and extremely stupid.

Finally, I think it is true that ideas emerge at a particular time. For example, the high conservatives are as anxious about the nature and effects of scientific culture as are the Marxists and radical thinkers. Indeed, the fact that we are all here discussing the problem is an expression of simultaneous discovery. Our ideas and misconceptions and confusions show that we are all attempting to grapple with a real and critical situation. The discussion of social ideas is always messier than a discussion of a particular technical area, and this muddle is a reflection of our society and its problems.

To return to Dr. Siekevitz's argument about the connection between science and technology, and the acceptance of the state's bribes by scientists: This worries me because sometimes the only thing to do is to get up and fight. And that isn't done on an individual basis; one has to do it with a lot of other people. In addition one has to get the ideas sorted out first.

In that sense, then, we have to learn to work together. The culture and training of science is highly individualistic, and, if anything, the training of sociologists is even more individualistic and competitive than that of natural scientists. Nevertheless, we must begin to view this intense individualism as something that actually stops us from sharing, and that prevents a common understanding of the problem. And without a common understanding of the problem, we cannot move to a common solution.

PART I. SCIENCE PUBLIC POLICY AS A FUNCTION OF
GOVERNMENT ORGANIZATION AND POLITICAL PHILOSOPHY

IN SEARCH OF A NATIONAL SCIENCE POLICY

Harold Fruchtbaum

School of Public Health
Columbia University
New York, New York 10032

The Honorable Emilio Q. Daddario, Chairman of the Subcommittee on Science, Research, and Development of the Committee on Science and Astronautics in the House of Representatives, opened what were to be fifteen days of hearings through the summer of 1970 on national science policy by offering reasons for the inquiry:

> First, upon careful perusal of congressional history we have found that no committee of the Congress has ever inquired precisely into this subject—although many have fielded parts of it in conjunction with other issues. Second, the Nation has clearly arrived at a point where the Government science relationship, which has been in a period of stability since World War II, is now faced with radical alteration. Under these circumstances, it is our intent to obtain the advice and views from a broad spectrum of Americans as to whether or not a structured national science policy is desirable in the future and, if so, what elements of that policy ought to be.[1]

Needless to say, after listening to 28 witnesses and reading the statements of 32 others—that "broad spectrum of Americans" drawn from government, industrial and university managements, science and scholarship—the Subcommittee concluded that "it is quite clear that our Nation is committed to the use of science and technology."

> In fact, the Federal Government is implicitly so charged by the Constitution which entrusts to it the responsibility to "establish justice, insure domestic tranquility, provide for the common defense, promote the general welfare"—none of which, however imperfectly innovated, could be possible without reliance upon science and technology.

The Subcommittee reasoned that if the government "has needed declared viable policy" for environment, welfare, space, labor, consumer protection, and health, it no less needed a defined policy for science, "the major instrument on which it must depend in contending with these and other matters."[2] (p. 3, 4).

Convinced there was a "suitable rationale" for attempting to establish a national science policy, the Subcommittee insisted on the recognition of two premises. First, the policy can only be promulgated by the federal government and in collaboration "with other government and nongovernment communities engaged in scientific activity," since "no other entity, public or private, has the purview, scope, or authority to undertake the task." Second,

> any national science policy cannot be considered separate and apart from national policy itself. That is to say, science policy must be part of and blend readily with the overall goals, objectives and priorities which are established by the American public through its duly constituted governmental process. Each policy is dependent upon the other.[2] (p. 5).

With the perspective of time the statement of the second condition may come to be seen as the Subcommittee's most significant contribution to the theory of science policy. Certainly, most of its recommendations have not been implemented. These included creating a special task force to draft a national science policy by the end of 1971; maintaining this policy as public law with continual review and reevaluation; incorporating the policy into the operations of each federal agency that uses science and technology in its mission; strengthening the Office of Science and Technology so that it can fulfill its statutory obligations; establishing the National Institutes of Research and Advanced Studies to consolidate federal responsibility for basic research and graduate study; developing stable funding procedures for scientific research; increasing the support of science education; inaugurating an up-to-date information system for managing the federal research and development enterprise; and preparing five-year projections of scientific and technological resources in relation to probable national needs. The Congressional Office of Technology Assessment proposed by the subcommittee did come into being, however[2] (p. 10–22).

What science policy there is remains what it has been throughout the two centuries of the Republic—ad hoc and, as the Subcommittee noted, neither enunciated nor necessarily permanent.[2] (p. 6, 7)

> At this time and, according to the committee's various studies and inquiries, at all prior times in our national history, the Government's science policy has been a patchwork response of attempting to apply some sort of scientific know-how in order to help solve particular issues or problems which could not be ignored or which seemed to have political appeal.[2] (p. 5).

To support this contention, the Subcommittee offered a 50-page history of federal science policy, such as it was, from 1787 to 1970,[2] (p. 65–115). No vestiges of comprehensive policies are to be found; rather, solutions were sought as problems requiring scientific knowledge arose or became politically unavoidable. Little more should be expected, it could be argued, for the genius of American politics lies in the muting of ideological differences, and if the price is piecemeal policy, then so be it. The cost would be far higher in the social and political struggle that would surely accompany any other approach. This position rests on two premises: (1) the economic situation is not so unfavorable that there is widespread discontent; (2) policy decisions in domestic and foreign affairs are accepted by the public as being in the national interest. If these conditions are not met, ideological conflict intensifies, and science policy, critical in the life of advanced industrial society, becomes a major area of dispute. "The present situation," the Congressmen concluded,

> contains the two essential elements which form the basis of need for a legally established national science policy. (1) The existence of severe problems which require the application of science and technology as at least part of their solution, and (2) A national capability, with adequate support, to supply and manage such applications with wisdom and dispatch.[2] (p. 8).

Defining a national science policy had to be left to others, but by listing what was wrong with the current ad hoc system, "an implied 'modus operandi'," the Subcommittee suggested what was needed.

> ... It does not begin to explain how things work with regard to priorities, the relationships between administrators and scientists, the problem of the poor versus the rich university or of geographical distribution. It does not attempt to describe the scientific estate or the "establishment," so-called—if there is

such a thing. It does not deal with the proper role of mission agencies in funding basic research. It does not describe in measured political terms what the Government thinks of science and technology, or how it intends to treat them.[2] (p. 6, 7).

Beyond calling for a national science policy and making recommendations for the improvement or creation of mechanisms for formulating it, the Subcommittee did not go. Neither did it wrestle with the implications of its own observation that national policy and national science policy are closely interrelated. In other words, the Subcommittee operated in the pragmatic and nontheoretical mode of congressional politics. The themes of the Subcommittee's hearings and report are familiar to historians of American science and government: ad hoc responses to particular problems and pressure groups, failed attempts to centralize the control of federal support for science and technology, superficial analyses of the implications of that support, unheeded calls for the formulation of national science policy. This history weighs heavily on those who seek fundamental change.

An Historical Perspective

Although the Constitution does not grant the federal government specific power to support science, the authority to do so is implied in the Preamble and Article I. Congress funded several technological undertakings that started to meet some of the new republic's needs: a patent system, the mint, weights and measures, health care for merchant seamen, geographical exploration, coast and geodetic surveys. But agriculture and higher education did not fare well in Congress. Proposals to aid the former were rejected, and plans for a national university died in the legislative process. Nevertheless, the federal government made some commitment to education by founding the Military Academy in 1802 at West Point. Active in topographical surveying before 1820, the War Department soon after turned to the improvement of river navigation and the construction of roads. The Navy created a Depot of Charts and Instruments in 1830 and four years later began an astronomical observatory.

Congressional support for such undertakings was not easily won. Unsure about the constitutionality of federal funding for internal improvements, Congress refused in 1845 to give Samuel F. B. Morse the money to extend his telegraph line from Baltimore to New York after he had used an initial appropriation of $30,000 to successfully demonstrate the system between Washington and Baltimore. Morse wanted the government to own the telegraph, but Congress stepped aside in favor of private enterprise. While Morse was having his difficulties with Congress, that body deliberated over what to do with the $500,000 left to the United States by the British scientist James Smithson to found in Washington, as he said in his will, "an Establishment for the increase and diffusion of knowledge among men." The ordeal of deciding went on intermittently from 1836 to 1845.

Up to the beginning of the Civil War in 1861, federal support for science and technology was spare, indeed. Only just emerging as professionals with specialized education and their own institutions and journals, scientists and engineers, with some notable exceptions, had little influence in Washington. Technical work useful to the military for fulfilling its role in opening new territories and protecting settlements as well as borders, coasts, and sea-lanes usually found support. The Civil War further stimulated the military's interest in technology. For example, the Union Navy experimented with ordnance and steam propulsion, and although the Army let go the opportunity to develop observation balloons, it did work on maintaining the health of troops and improving the care of battle casualties. The Secretary of War established the Sanitary Commission, appointing physicians and scientists to oversee hygienic conditions in military camps and hospitals and to operate a system of relief aid for soldiers and their families. Confederate activity followed similar lines but with different emphases.

Leading scientists and scientist-administrators like Alexander Dallas Bache, director of the Coast Survey, and Joseph Henry, secretary of the Smithsonian Institution, gave their services to the Union. With Charles Henry Davis, head of the Bureau of Navigation, they made up the Navy Department's Permanent Commission, which was formed to advise the government on "all subjects of a scientific character...."* Although not a research organization but rather a valuator of the ideas and proposals submitted to it, the Commission was the closest approximation to a central agency for science during the Civil War. From these experiences some scientists learned the role of the influential in Washington. A number of them, such as Bache, had already concluded that the advance of American science depended to a significant extent on support from the government. In return, scientists would provide information and advice about technological problems, perhaps creating an institution for the purpose. Working with Senator Henry Wilson of Massachusetts, Bache, Davis, Louis Agassiz, and others achieved this end when Congress passed a bill in March 1863, on the last day of the session, establishing the National Academy of Sciences. Five committees were formed to assist the government with technical matters, but the Academy lost its momentum a year before the war's end when Bache, the prime mover, fell ill.

The history of the industrial and agricultural expansion in the years after the Civil War cannot be reviewed here, but with this enormous technological development important laboratories and research bureaus came into being under the aegis of several departments in the Executive Branch. By 1884 proposals for the creation of a cabinet Department of Science to centralize the administration of the government's scientific activity were being made. The influential Alexander Agassiz argued that not only would such a department be appropriate, but also, in keeping with the spirit of laissez-faire, "the Government should limits its support of science to such work as is within neither the province nor the capacity of the individual or of the universities, or of associations and scientific societies."[4] Nevertheless, a centralized administration for science failed to attract sufficient support to become a reality. The desire of departments to keep control of their technical bureaus and the fear of the proposed organization's potential power were insurmountable obstacles.

Faced with the growing possibility that the United States would enter the European war, the federal government implemented a policy of preparedness in 1916 by creating the Council of National Defense to promote the coordination of essential resources and industries. The Council evolved into the War Industries Board and the Food Administration, both powerful agencies of economic control. The Navy, with the precedent of its Permanent Commission from the Civil War, established the Consulting Board composed of notable engineers and inventors chaired by Thomas Alva Edison. Several members of the National Academy of Sciences sought to revitalize that venerable institution by offering its services to the government. Urged on by the astronomer, George Ellery Hale, the Academy made a proposal of this kind to President Woodrow Wilson in April 1916, and on his accept-

---

* See Reference 3. After two decades, Dupree's book is still an invaluable guide and has been helpful in the development of my perspective.

ance organized the National Research Council with representatives from science, industry, and education. By the end of the war, the NRC had become a major scientific agency.

Military innovations like poison gas, submarine warfare, and armored vehicles combined with the need for efficient industrial and agricultural production brought scientists and engineers to prominence. The First World War underscored the value of industrial research and gave many scientists their first experience in large-scale research and development. A number of them, especially Hale and Robert A. Millikan, took from their war work the lesson that an important function of science is to buttress democracy. In the spirit of early twentieth-century progressivism, they claimed the objective or scientific method indispensable for the operation of honest and efficient government. "Indeed," Millikan said, "I regard the development and spread of this method as the most important contribution of science to life for *it represents the only hope of the race of ultimately getting out of the jungle.*"[5]†

Many American social and natural scientists and engineers in the 1920's accepted as one of their professional responsibilities the promotion of efficiency. Secretary of Commerce Herbert Hoover exemplified that position. Through such agencies as the Bureau of Standards, his Department worked to increase what he understood to be the efficiency of the American economy. In public addresses he stressed the importance of research for industry, and launched in April 1926 the National Research Fund to raise money from business for basic science. The Fund, a complete failure, died quietly in 1934. Millikan and others who believed in the ideal of a national science that fostered democracy and social efficiency were brought by the disaster of the Great Depression to doubt the future of democracy when the people were inadequately educated in the scientific method.

Toward the end of the election campaign of 1932, President Hoover said, "we are yet but on the frontiers of development of science, and of invention."[7] Science and technology as frontiers—how American a metaphor!—would find varied use during the Depression and in the years after the Second World War. Recognition within the administration of President Franklin Delano Roosevelt that planning policy and research policy could have a useful relationship led to the creation of the National Resources Board in 1934. Its successor, the National Resources Committee, undertook a study of the place of research in the federal government. As Roosevelt put it, "research is one of the Nation's very greatest resources and the role of the Federal Government in supporting and stimulating it needs to be reexamined."[8] The three-volume report, *Research—A National Resource,* surveyed the relation of the federal government, industry, and business to research, and was the most extensive undertaking of its kind to that date in the United States. Despite a series of recommendations for improving the administration and support of research within the government and for enhancing the cooperation between public and private agencies, no explicit national science policy was proposed by the National Resources Committee. What science policy there was remained ad hoc, ill-defined, and decentralized.

Although a comprehensive national science policy did not exist, at least two areas of research received support from the federal government in the late 1930s. Congressional authorization of funds for basic research within the Department of Agriculture enabled it to create regional laboratories, each concentrating on specific problems, a departure from the older system of state-by-state experimental

---

† For a detailed historical analysis see Reference 6.

stations. The Department established the primary center for its scientific work in Beltsville, Maryland. Innovations were also made in financing public health and medical research. The Social Security Act of 1935 provided money for state and local health agencies through the Public Health Service, a new departure in federal policy. With the creation of the National Cancer Institute in 1937, funds for research and the further training of scientists were channeled into the study of a major disease problem, the beginning of the federal government's long-term commitment to the support of the medical sciences.

The United States entered the Second World War without a formulated science policy, but the conflict demonstrated the value of research and the organization of the nation's technical resources. One legacy of the war was the resurrection of the idea that a central agency for furthering science was needed. After three years of Congressional hearings and study, Senator Harley M. Kilgore of West Virginia proposed the creation of a National Research Foundation to increase and coordinate the government's support of work "in fields that are predominantly in the public interests, notably national defense, health and medical care, and the basic sciences"; to stimulate research in private institutions; to promote the rapid introduction and use of new discoveries. Kilgore specified that at least 20 percent of the Foundation's funds should be earmarked for military research and a like amount for the health and medical sciences.[9, 10]

Vannevar Bush, director of the wartime Office of Scientific Research and Development, recommended a National Research Foundation in his report of July 1945, *Science, the Endless Frontier,* written in response to a request from President Roosevelt dated November 17, 1944. Roosevelt had asked for proposals about disseminating the technical knowledge developed during the war, fostering the medical sciences, aiding the research activities of public and private agencies, and discovering and developing the scientific talent of American youth. Roosevelt wrote:

> New frontiers of the mind are before us, and if they are pioneered with the same vision, boldness, and drive with which we have waged this war we can create a fuller and more fruitful employment and a fuller and more fruitful life.[11]

Bush and his colleagues wanted an agency that would "develop and promote a national policy for scientific research and scientific education," stimulate research in nonprofit organizations, provide training grants, and "by contract and otherwise support long-range research on military matters." Bush urged placing in the Foundation "the responsibilities for civilian-initiated and civilian-controlled military research," while

> the job of long-range research involving application of the newest scientific discoveries to military needs should be the responsibility of those civilian scientists in the universities and in industry who are best trained to discharge it thoroughly and successfully.[12]

In testimony before several congressional committees, he emphasized the science-military connection. As Bush told the House Committee on Military Affairs, "in keeping this Nation vigorously able to defend itself, there is no more important factor than that of scientific research enthusiastically and energetically pursued."[13, 14] The National Science Foundation Act of 1950, passed and signed into law after nearly five years of effort, stipulated that one of the new agency's functions was "at the request of the Secretary of Defense, to initiate and support specific scientific research activities in connection with matters relating to the national defense...."[15] (p. 267, 268).

SCIENCE POLICY AND SOCIAL JUSTICE

The Act of 1950 authorized and directed the National Science Foundation "to develop and encourage the pursuit of a national policy for the promotion of basic research and education in the sciences."[12] (p. 267). Here the NSF has failed. In the pages of Congressional hearings and reports and in documents from executive agencies are found only fragments of science policies, and for the most part these were responses to what were seen as crises.

We will not be able to design and implement a coherent national science policy until we develop in a truly democratic way a coherent national policy. This will require great effort over a considerable period of time. The complexity of the problem can be suggested as follows. American policies supposedly rest on the assumption that they promote the general welfare. Imagine, however, the general welfare defined in terms of John Rawls' theory of justice: "All social values—liberty and opportunity, income and wealth, and the bases of self-respect—are to be distributed equally unless an unequal distribution of any, or all, of these values is to everyone's advantage."[16] How would our national science policy, such as it is, and the national policy from which it derives have to be changed to meet Rawls' definition? In the answer are the seeds of a social revolution.

REFERENCES

1. U. S. HOUSE OF REPRESENTATIVES. 1970. National Science Policy. Hearings before the Subcommittee on Science, Research, and Development of the Committee on Science and Astronautics, 91st Congress, 2d Session, July 7–September 17, 1970: 2.
2. U. S. HOUSE OF REPRESENTATIVES. 1970. Toward a Science Policy for the United States. Report of the Subcommittee on Science, Research, and Development to the Committee on Science and Astronautics, 91st Congress, 2d Session, October 15, 1970.
3. WELLES, G. February 11, 1863. Letter to Charles Henry Davis. Quoted in: DUPREE, A. H. 1957. Science in the Federal Government: A History of Policies and Activities to 1940: 137. Harvard University Press. Cambridge, Mass.
4. [AGASSIZ, A.] 1885. The national government and science. The Nation **41**: 526.
5. MILLIKAN, R. A. 1928. Science and modern life. *In* The Creative Intelligence and Modern Life. F. J. McConnell, *et al.*: 159. University of Colorado. Boulder, Colorado.
6. TOBEY, R. C. 1971. The American Ideology of National Science, 1919–1930: 167–198. University of Pittsburgh Press. Pittsburgh, Pa.
7. HOOVER, H. 1932. *In* The State Papers and Other Public Writings of Herbert Hoover. 1934. W. S. Myers, Ed. Vol. 2:423–424. Doubleday, Doran. Garden City, N.Y.
8. ROOSEVELT, F. D. July 19, 1937. *In* Research—A National Resource. Relation of the Federal Government to Research. November 1938. Report of the Science Committee to the National Resources Committee. Vol. 1:2. U. S. Government Printing Office. Washington, D.C.
9. U. S. HOUSE OF REPRESENTATIVES. 1970. Toward a Science Policy for the United States. Report of the Subcommittee on Science, Research, and Development to the Committee on Science and Astronautics, 91st Congress, 2d Session, October 15, 1970: 83.
10. U. S. SENATE. 1945. Hearings on Science Legislation (S. 1297 and Related Bills). Opening Statement by Senator Harley M. Kilgore. Hearings before a Subcommittee of the Committee on Military Affairs, 79th Congress, 1st Session, October 8, 1945: 1–6.
11. ROOSEVELT, F. D. November 17, 1944. *In* Bush[12] (pp. 3, 4).
12. BUSH, V. July 1945. Science, the Endless Frontier. Reprinted July 1960: 34. National Science Foundation. Washington, D.C.

13. U. S. HOUSE OF REPRESENTATIVES. 1945. Research and Development. Hearings before the Committee on Military Affairs, 79th Congress, 1st Session, May 22–29, 1945: 3.
14. U. S. HOUSE OF REPRESENTATIVES. 1947. National Science Foundation. Hearings before the Committee on Interstate and Foreign Commerce, 80th Congress, 1st Session, March 6–7, 1947: 246–247.
15. U. S. HOUSE OF REPRESENTATIVES. 1966. The National Science Foundation: A General Review of Its First 15 Years. Report of the Committee on Science and Astronautics. House Document No. 317. 89th Congress, 2d Session, January 24, 1966.
16. RAWLS, J. 1971. A Theory of Justice: 62. Harvard University Press. Cambridge, Mass.

DISCUSSION

LESTER TALKINGTON: I would like to know more about Millikan's final conclusion, which you characterize as conservative.

DR. FRUCHTBAUM: By 1938, if not before, he had come to the conclusion that the future of American society required the formulation of national policies by juries of scientists selected by their peers. These scientific juries would study social problems, determine the relevant facts, and devise appropriate solutions. So he had moved from the progressive's faith in democracy to a conservative trust in rule by a scientific oligarchy.

JOSEPH BERNSTEIN: The story of the evolution of public policy in science is incomplete without noting this change: there has been a more definitive role of the government in controlling scientific work. For example, there is the recent moratorium on research on the live fetus. There is also control over the introduction of new drugs by the F.D.A., which has its good, bad, and neutral aspects. Some claim that this overcontrol of scientific research prevents the introduction of good drugs that are already available elsewhere. This is one point that illustrates the dynamic interplay between government and science.

DR. FRUCHTBAUM: There's no question that the implications of this interplay are important, as we already see in the biomedical sciences. For example, new ethical issues in health care are beginning to influence public policy, and they are being felt in undergraduate and medical education. But without a defined national science policy derived from a defined national policy, the social and philosophical problems of science, medicine, and technology will be even more difficult to resolve. This is indeed troubling, given the many recent examples of the inhumane use of innovations from these fields.

AARON POSNER: Actually, in point of fact, we do have de facto government support of research because very little basic research is done outside of the aegis of the government. Do we want highly centralized support? Are you implying that we need greater organization of that government support?

DR. FRUCHTBAUM: I want a reformulation of national policies founded on a new vision of American society and then the creation of a national science policy compatible with this vision. In the history of these policies, such as they are, one seldom sees this question raised: do they promote social justice?

DR. POSNER: I'm afraid I'm going to be classed with Millikan at this point! I believe that we *do* have a policy that is thought out, especially the NIH policy, which Dr. Sherman will undoubtedly speak to, but our policy is formless in the sense that we leave it to the basic scientists who apply for money to decide where we're going. So what you're saying, Dr. Fruchtbaum, is that we should have political goals that determine what our science is working towards. Dr. Bernstein brought up the point that we have a political problem now—research on the fetus—and so political input is put into science. Sometimes we agree with it and sometimes we don't.

DR. FRUCHTBAUM: My concern is how those policies are made, who makes them, what mechanisms exist for democratic participation in the decision process. At present these mechanisms are very limited and quite faulty, and that worries me. I think we are very close to agreement in one sense: there is a science policy of sorts and it does serve a political end. I am concerned about the nature of that end.

J. BELLAVIA: It seems to me that your basic point is that there should be a more centralized or specific concept of polity and you wish to consider how scientists might help to implement that polity in a structured way. I would like to suggest that the only way that this might be done is by the efforts of the scientific community. Perhaps the scientific community itself is not centralized enough. Because there are so many branches of science, individual scientists are more or less involved in their own area, and not working together as aware citizens to coordinate their efforts to institute a better polity.

DR. FRUCHTBAUM: It's unfortunate that not everyone was present last night to hear the paper by Hilary and Steven Rose. I would like to tie my remarks into it, because one of the points they made, and I think rightly, is that the scientific community consists of a small elite directing a mass of scientific workers. How policy is made within that community and how democratic the process needs to be considered. American science policy from the nineteenth century to the present has been made by a small number of men such as Agassiz, Bache, Davis, Henry and a few others. Of course, the group of scientific "influentials" grew as the nation grew and the investment in science and technology increased, but relatively speaking, it is a small group. I think it is important that we not work on the assumption that science is a participatory democracy in which each scientist has an equal voice and an equal vote in policy-making. That's a mistake we make, with some very painful consequences as we have seen in the last three decades.

Ms. BELLAVIA: It then becomes important to reassess the scientific community. At least there is some awareness of the problem. Changes are going to have to be made here, and then move on up. The groundwork for change has to be within the scientific community.

DR. FRUCHTBAUM: I agree. In a number of laboratories in this country, there are people working toward real change, even in the way laboratories operate. It is hoped that this will have an important social and political impact, but it remains to be seen.

PUBLIC AND PRIVATE SECTOR INSTITUTIONS: THEIR INTERACTING ROLES IN SETTING PUBLIC POLICY

John Foord Sherman

*Association of American Medical Colleges
One Dupont Circle, N.W.
Washington, D.C. 20036*

In his remarkably insightful observations of the United States in the 1830s, Alexis de Tocqueville marveled at the extent to which the citizens of our new country used extragovernmental organizations to serve a variety of purposes.

> ...Americans of all ages, all conditions, all dispositions, constantly form associations. They have not only commercial and manufacturing companies, in which all take part, but associations of a thousand other kinds—religious, moral, serious, futile, general or restricted, enormous or diminutive....
> If it be proposed to inculcate some truth, or to foster some feeling by the encouragement of a great example, they form a society. Wherever, at the head of some new undertaking, you see the government in France, or a man of rank in England, in the United States you will be sure to find an association...[1]

Thus, while many of the public and private institutions relating to scientific enterprise in the United States have counterparts in other scientifically developed countries, the role or influence of these counterparts frequently varies significantly from that in our country. One can state with considerable confidence that several aspects of the national character, the perception of which prompted de Tocqueville to write those words, have given rise to the circumstance of the prominent interacting roles that will be examined in this paper. Further, we may speculate that the current era may be one of the greatest importance insofar as the sum of those interactions determines the vigor and direction of the nation's scientific efforts and their contributions to the public good. We seem largely to have emerged from the recent period of almost complete disillusionment with science, its practitioners, and its results, but we are about to enter another period where for the first time in our nation's history the prevailing faith in America's unlimited resources and ingenuity to assure the conquest of any national problem will be put to its severest test. As in any time of threat to our national security, our citizens and their political representatives will turn to the scientists and technologists for some leadership and much assistance. Now we are concerned about areas where the issues and their solutions lie only partially within the ability of those specialists to produce definitive answers. In this instance the primary threat to our national security lies for the first time largely within ourselves. Unless the institutions, public and private, which are the subject of this conference rise adequately to meet their responsibilities for this awesome task, I fear that we may find ourselves repeating that famous utterance of Walt Kelly's Pogo, "We have met the enemy and they is us."

With that beginning, I should like to discuss this particular topic along the following lines:

1. To review briefly the history of the diversity and character of the public and private institutions which in their interactions have shaped United States public policy in scientific matters.

2. To examine in some detail one sector of the national scientific endeavor,

namely, biomedical research. While that field differs significantly from others in certain respects, there are sufficient points of commonality, I believe, for it to be a useful and acceptable example.

3. Finally, to offer some personal observations as to what might be the most appropriate approach in the private and governmental sectors to promote and facilitate the advancement of the public good.

Given the experience of the founding fathers with colonial rule, it is not surprising that the earliest efforts concerning domestic scientific matters in this young nation should involve organizations that were nongovernmental or at most quasi-governmental in character. Nor is it any wonder that under the circumstances of that time, such bodies emphasized the natural sciences. The first truly scientific society in this country was the American Philosophical Society, founded during the 1740s under Benjamin Franklin's stimulus. Although decidedly intellectual in character, its purpose stressed the "useful arts."[2] The assessment of organizations or activities primarily on the basis of their presumed utilitarian worth was as pronounced in that era as it is today, if not more so. Indeed, one part of the Constitution recognized both the importance of extragovernmental loci of scientific undertakings as well as the necessity of incentives to stimulate practical application. Article 1, Section 8 of the Constitution provides that: "The Congress shall have power to promote the progress of science and the useful arts by securing to authors and inventors the exclusive right to their respective writings and discoveries."

In this context, then, it is understandable, for example, that the strong desire to exploit the vast natural resources of the new land stimulated an early and deep interest in surveys of the country and its untapped wealth. Such studies were recognized as an essential first step to that end. Thus we learn of the establishment in 18 of the Columbian Institute in Washington. Shyrock describes this organization as designed "... to bring statesmen and scientists together in the quest of utilitarian values."[3] As with many of its lineal and nonlineal successors of that era, the Institute failed to survive the lack of interest by both the Federal government and wealthy potential benefactors. It is ironic, in that the Federal government would shortly be forced to turn to the nation's scientists and technologists for assistance in the conduct of the Civil War. And many men of means were profiting even then on the fruits of the meager research and development activities underway at home but particularly abroad. Notable exceptions to this state of national indifference during the period were the Congressionally established Smithsonian Institution and the privately founded American Society of Geologists, the latter subsequently to be a nucleus of the American Association for the Advancement of Science when it was formed in the late 1840s. Even the Smithsonian, as an exception, required a gestation period of almost ten years during which a very reluctant Congress debated whether or not to accept James Smithson's bequest for its establishment.

The almost "total war" nature of the prosecution of the Civil War by the Federal government prompted recognition of the potential contributions of science and technology as forces to be cultivated for the advancement of the public interest. Most significantly, the establishment in 1863 of the National Academy of Sciences presaged a continuum of new organizations inside and outside of government that had as the major if not sole raison d'être the advancement of a scientific or technological cause or the provision of research support. During all of this period of development, the extent and quality of exchanges between the public and private sector grew considerably in almost every dimension.

Some of the most fascinating chapters in the history of our country are those that describe the manner in which public and private agencies, sometimes in concert, at other times in competition or outright disagreement, stimulated, supported, protected, and used the nation's maturing research and development enterprise often in the public interest but at times for selfish purposes. Many historians and other observers have reviewed in considerable detail specific areas of science and technology. They range from Don Price's partial analysis of the nation's oceanography program[4] to a case study of the infamous AD-X2 battery additive incident.[5] Other writers have placed such specific instances in perspective as they examine the sweep of American history in the context of science and technology. Although such overall examinations cannot describe in detail the nature, extent, or even identification of the various organizations that were influential as those developments occurred, source documents do. I believe it safe to assert that all national research policies in this country have been established as a result of inputs from multiple sources. Those sources now include:

I. Public
   A. Federal Government
      1. Executive Branch
         a. Office of Management and Budget
         b. Operating agencies
         c. Regulatory agencies
         d. Science and Technology Policy Office
      2. Legislative Branch
         a. Legislative committees
         b. Appropriation committees
         c. Oversight committees
         d. Joint committees
         e. Office of Technology Assessment
      3. Judicial Branch
   B. Regional authorities
   C. State and local governments
II. Private
   A. Academic institutions
   B. Industrial and commercial organizations
   C. Academies, associations, and societies
   D. Foundations
   E. Voluntary agencies
   F. General and specialized news media
   G. Public interest law firms
   H. Organized religious groups
   I. Labor unions

To a surprising degree a variety of individual institutions and organizations among the array listed above play an increasingly influential and usually constructive role in policy development. The policy-maker, politician, or agency official who does not recognize that probability finds himself in considerable difficulty.

With this necessarily superficial overview of the subject, let us now examine in some detail the field of biomedical research. I have selected this area as an example for two reasons. First, it is one in which I spent more than twenty exciting and rewarding years as an official at the National Institutes of Health. Second, and more important, I believe that it offers unique opportunities for both retrospective and prospective studies of importance for that field as well as for extrapolation elsewhere. Except for the military in time of war or possibly energy in the immediate future, no other field of research and development claims so much attention nationally nor is influenced in its policies by a larger number or greater diversity of institutions.

In contrast to that of other scientific fields, the early history of biomedical research in this country was characterized by indifference from the public as well as the medical profession. In his excellent history of American medical research, Shyrock wrote of the antebellum period

> Since research was then focused on the identification of diseases (pure science) rather than on their treatment (applied science), the results that might please a physician were of small concern to the public. [To make matters worse]... the successful practitioner was admired for both his wealth and his services, but there was little interest in research, an occupation that had little monetary value and brought no immediate benefits.[6]

Interestingly, the post-Civil War precedents established in agriculture were of particular but largely indirect importance to the growth of biomedical research.[7] Government support was initiated for both research and the education system (land-grant colleges) as a result of pressures from agrarian interests. The concept of research grants to nonfederal institutions was developed and experience was gained in the problems of working with Congress and of administering such programs. Even advances in medicine resulted from these broadly conceived and implemented activities. However, most of the biomedical research that was undertaken was carried out by a few physicians in the major medical schools, and largely at their own expense. It required a combination of the reforms in American medical education led by Welch and later Flexner with major advances in the understanding and treatment of infectious diseases, largely drawn from European sources to finally provide a basis for the biomedical research enterprise that now flourishes in this country. And one notes that during that entire century both advances in the cause of biomedical research and obstacles to its progress were the consequences of already emergent influences that were shaping what became national if not public policy. The list even then is extensive, and I shall identify but a few—the Marine Hospital Service (now part of the United States Public Health Service), the Departments of War and Navy as well as Agriculture, the Congress, the practicing medical profession and its American Medical Association, druggists who founded today's older pharmaceutical firms, and a small but determined number of individuals, both lay and professional. Despite a continuing but slow rate of growth until after World War II, the base for what would become world leadership in this field was firmly established and the pattern by which public policy would be developed was clearly discernible.

Where, then, are we at present? The most recent estimate of expenditures for biomedical research and development in this country was of the order of $3.5 billion in 1973, of which $2.2 billion came from federal appropriations, $1.0 billion from industrial and commercial sources, and the balance from a variety of private sources, particularly foundations and voluntary health agencies.[8] More than 3,000 institutions and organizations carry on research programs with these funds and probably 50,000 to 60,000 scientists are involved.[9] The keystone of this vast undertaking, of course, is the National Institutes of Health, with its sizeable and renowned intramural research program and the very extensive extramural sponsorship through thousands of grants and contracts to nonfederal institutions and organizations. Any enterprise of this magnitude deserves considerable attention as to its productiveness, vigor, management, and coherency. I can assure you from personal experience that the attention is continuous, from a variety of both public and private sources. Despite that constant attempt at overview, it is not a simple matter to assess the total effort in the context of those important characteristics. Nonetheless, it is in this task that I believe the pluralistic system, which involves the interaction of numerous public and private institutions, performs its most important and valuable function.

Before further elaboration on that personal conclusion and others of a related nature, I believe it would be helpful to examine in some detail the types of institutions in question and the nature of their involvement. A number of excellent volumes[10-23] have been written about science and public policy, and in the biomedical area, four[3, 21-23] deserve special attention, and I refer you to them for historical fact. In the interest of time, I shall use a hypothetical case with an unidentified research area as the focal point. While ficititious, I believe it to be entirely reasonable and, therefore, acceptable for illustrative purposes. It is as follows:

At some of those unique Washington cocktail parties, aides to members of Congress speculated from time to time on the increasing numbers of inquiries their legislators were receiving concerning a hitherto undiscussed illness affecting infants in various parts of the country. Information obtained from the National Institutes of Health indicated that some research on the problem was underway in two or three of the Institutes as well as in an institute funded by two private foundations. However, its incidence was seemingly low and little was known about it. Simultaneously, numbers of parents in different geographic areas conferred in anguish with their physicians and clergy as they watched helplessly while their firstborn children struggled, often unsuccessfully, to survive. The practitioners consulting with their colleagues at nearby medical centers were told that little more in the way of diagnosis or treatment was available. Consultations became more frequent and intensive and together with autopsy reports, relevant data slowly accumulated. The Center for Disease Control in Atlanta, while still studying the situation, especially from an epidemiological point of view, tentatively concluded that no infectious agent was involved. Similarly, the Food and Drug Administration, continuing to monitor reports of adverse drug reactions, also tentatively concluded that no pattern existed to warrant postulating a drug-induced cause.

These developments, of course, occurred over a period of many months, during which time the number of cases continued to increase. Since it was not a reportable disease, an accurate assessment as to the extent of its morbidity and mortality became extremely difficult. With medical science and local practitioners unable to help, parents of stricken children grasped at the hope offered by advertisements placed in local papers and magazines by a small firm offering a device which purported to support the infant during the critical period of the illness. Irate physicians, who had good reason to be skeptical of the claims for the device, soon prompted an investigation by the Federal Trade Commission. The predictably lengthy process of hearings, findings, and appeals commenced. As more attention was drawn to the syndrome, especially among parents and physicians, two further developments occurred. Comparing experiences at PTA meetings, after church services and at social gatherings, the growing numbers of parents, relatives, and friends whose lives were affected by the malady found not only a common bond but also a cause requiring action on their part. From a scattering of loosely organized groups in various cities and towns, there evolved in a brief span of years one of de Tocqueville's American associations. This one was dedicated solely to the purpose of gaining local and national support for research on and treatment of the affliction. Well-informed, persistent volunteers compared notes, developed materials, held meetings and pressed their cause among legislatures, the media, the research centers and agencies and practicing physicians. Meantime, the baffled and targeted doctors and scientists, having run numerous leads to unproductive conclusions, had been organized by the Director of the National Institute of Child Health and Human Development, NIH, into an ad hoc committee to review the state of knowledge and to make recommendations as to how to expand the small and only slowly growing research program.

Following on these developments, a classic but predictable confrontation occurred. Stimulated by hearing from ever larger numbers of impatient parents and others, members of the Congress prompted hearings by appropriate committees to determine what more could be done. Dissatisfied with what they considered bureaucratic excuses and conservatism on the part of Administration witnesses, legislators introduced bills in both Houses of Congress to establish a separate Institute within the NIH dedicated solely to research on this affliction. Testimony in favor of the legislation was provided by the newly appointed, full-time Director of the Association, with eloquent assistance from several parents, physicians, and scientists. Not surprisingly the Administration witnesses opposed the legislation as unnecessary and duplicative of general authorities already provided by the Congress. They cited the slowly but definitely expanding research program already underway, the conferences and discussions by the NIH program staff to seek new ideas and recruit additional investigators into that field, the lack of applications for grant support and, most importantly, the definite paucity of good research leads. It was also pointed out that additional Institutes were costly not just in money but particularly in personnel at a time when efforts were underway to reduce the size of the federal workforce. Nonetheless, the legislation passed by sizeable margins.

By pure coincidence and as a result of intensive efforts by a variety of groups, some of which were religious in nature, legislation imposing a sweeping ban on research involving pregnant women and infants was under consideration. Thus, another classic confrontation was developing around considerations of ethics. Ironically, the legislation covered one of the few aspects of the expanding research program which was beginning to display some promise.

I could continue at length with this recital, describing how:

(1) the Office of Management and Budget required a reduction in the dollar and personnel resources for the new Institute in the face of a budget crisis which occurred shortly after the President signed the legislation authorizing the new research program;

(2) another national association sued successfully to block the OMB reduction in funds;

(3) a public interest law firm attempted through the courts to terminate the long-standing confidentiality of protocols in research grant applications, alleging that the rights of infants were being infringed upon in some grant-supported research;

(4) rather searching hearings were held by a Congressional oversight committee when it appeared that under external pressures to expand the program, the NIH had made some awards without true peer review;

(5) and finally, there was an unusual expression of concern by the National Academy of Sciences that the magnitude and nature of the now sizeable research

program had seriously outrun its knowledge base and questioned the proposal to appropriate even more money for it.

I believe, however, the prior recitation has made my point. Science policy in this country is the result of a continuous, fragmented, slow-moving, often frustrating and sometimes paradoxical, if not actually internally contradictory, process. It can be inefficient in its allocation and expenditure of resources. Like the scientific activities that it governs, it is often unpredictable. Despite these shortcomings and the need for improvements in the process, I suggest that because of the nature and importance of the enterprise it shapes, that process does serve the country reasonably well.

To support that contention, I would like to review briefly what I believe to be some of the advantages as well as several disadvantages of our pluralistic system, as based on this complex interaction of public and private institutions. As for the advantages:

1. The present approach preserves the important shared public-private character of the policy development process, thus protecting against the possibility of domination by either public or private interests. Experience from other countries, such as Germany under Hitler, together with the nature of our own traditions and culture make this approach as important in the area of science policy as in other aspects of our national life.

2. The interaction between public and private institutions tends to increase the efficiency and effectiveness of each party or each type of institution as they carry out their respective responsibilities. This is no small advantage given the sometimes inefficient nature of research itself due to its unpredictability.

3. This arrangement both fosters and protects the open nature of the scientific operation. For example, despite the fact that the NIH system of peer review for assessment of grant applications and contract proposals operates under a system of confidentiality, the sheer number of individuals drawn from the private sector which constitutes that system assures a degree of accountability that would not be the case were only government employees involved.

4. The interaction assures the availablity and utilization of the highest degree and greatest variety of scientific expertise in the decision-making process. Again, referring to peer review as used by many government science agencies, the individuals selected for that task are chosen for their technical expertise rather than for institutional affiliation, political point of view, or other considerations.

5. This approach facilitates the communication process both within the scientific community and for the public at large. Given the problems of communication within the scientific community as well as the ever-present difficulty of informing the public and their Congressional representatives as to progress in biomedical research and the limitations on it as well as opportunities that lie ahead, this particular advantage is also of considerable moment.

At the same time we must openly recognize and admit possible disadvantages:

1. As is clearly illustrated by the history of most scientific activities in this country, the policies governing those activities as well as the level and allocation of resources may be unduly influenced by the very special interest groups contributing to that policy development. Although it is to be hoped that the ultimate outcome accrues unquestionably to the public interest, there is no built-in assurance that this will occur.

2. Given the complexity of the issues and the haste with which such matters unfold and are decided, the multifaceted approach to the development of science policy may well result in less than sufficient and enlightened debate of the issues. With a variety of positions espoused by different groups clamoring to be heard, it frequently becomes difficult to select the real signals because of the high level of background noise.

3. As the stakes rise, particularly in the allocations of resources, the possibility of competition among the various types of public and private sector institutions dominating policy development can well result in those policies evolving by default rather than by a more rational process.

I would reiterate that despite these dangers and the accompanying confusion or less than perfect outcome of the pluralistic process, I believe strongly that it is to be preferred to a semimonolithic system implied by such suggestions as that for the establishment of a Department of Science. Although no doubt a degree of public-private exchange would continue, the gains in efficiency of the decision-making process would in my belief be seriously offset by possible decreases in the effectiveness of the programs to be carried out. For example, given the still utilitarian outlook of our society and culture, it appears that the needs of science are better served by relating research sponsorship to particular social purposes. Those purposes in turn are better served by providing a strong, fundamental science base for the more applied activities representing the ultimate purpose. The history of advances both in modern medicine and the National Institutes of Health provides ample evidence for those statements. An essential exception to this hypothesis is, of course, the non-mission-oriented role of the National Science Foundation.

This state of affairs, however, does suggest strongly the need for better coordinating capabilities at the highest levels of government. The waning of influence and subsequent elimination of the Office of Science and Technology and the President's Science Advisory Committee have left a major void which is only partially filled by the Science and Technology Policy Office, currently a component of the National Science Foundation. In this context, it is to be hoped that the recent report by the National Academy of Sciences' committee under the chairmanship of James R. Killian will be given serious consideration by the present Administration, the Congress, and the scientific community.[24] As you are probably aware, the committee recommended that a "Council on Science and Technology" be established, analagous to the Council of Economic Advisors. It is well-recognized that no advisory apparatus will be maximally useful unless the person to be advised desires it. Nonetheless, it would seem that the experience subsequent to the demise of OST has convinced numbers of people that a stronger arrangement is desirable. Such a Council together with a prestigious, highly objective staff could provide a new degree of usefulness, resulting in receptivity in the White House. To carry out its responsibilities, the Congress also requires access to objective scientific expertise. The new Office of Technology Assessment may provide that capability although the experience with it to date is too brief to permit a judgment to be made.

In summary, I would like once again to speak strongly in behalf of the currently pluralistic system of science policy development in this country, based on the complex of interactions between various public and private institutions. Such a conclusion recognizes its imperfections and the need for constant improvement. The uncertainties that lie immediately ahead associated with the energy, materials, and financial crises added to the always-present scientific responsibilities and challenges, make all the more important the need for reexamination by those institutions of their responsibilities in this process. In particular, I would suggest a requirement for greater self-discipline on the part of two of the major components of that process: the federal government and the scientific community. The former must recognize the necessity of avoiding actions that impose unrealistic expectations or limitations on our scientific enterprise. The latter must avoid making exaggerated promises or neglecting perceived societal goals. Unless those conditions obtain, I fear we will fail to serve our own interests properly, to say nothing of the overriding public good.

REFERENCES

1. DE TOCQUEVILLE, A. 1964. Democracy in America. R. Gilpin and C. Wright, Eds. Science and National Policy-Making. Columbia University Press. New York, N.Y.
2. VAN DOREN, C. 1938. Benjamin Franklin.: 139. Viking Press. New York, N.Y.
3. SHYROCK, R. H. 1947. American Medical Research.: 26. The Commonwealth Fund. New York, N.Y.
4. PRICE, D. K. 1965. The Scientific Estate. Chapt. 7. Harvard University Press. Cambridge, Mass.
5. LAWRENCE, S. A. 1962. The Battery Additive Controversy in Case Studies in American Government. E. A. Bock and A. K. Campbell, Eds.: 325–368. Prentice-Hall. Englewood, N.J.
6. SHYROCK, R. H. *op. cit.*: 31.
7. *Ibid.*: 42–43.
8. Basic Data Relating to the National Institutes of Health. 1974. U.S. Department of Health Education and Welfare.: 3. Washington, D.C.
9. ROSENBERG, H. H. (Policy Studies Officer, Office of Program and Planning and Evaluation, NIH.) Personal communication.
10. BUSH, V. 1945. Science: The Endless Frontier. U.S. Office of Scientific Research and Development. Washington, D.C.
11. BROOKS, H. 1968. The Government of Science. MIT Press. Cambridge, Mass.
12. GREENBERG, D. S. 1967. The Politics of Pure Science. American Library Association. New York, N.Y.
13. KIDD, C. V. 1959. American Universities and Federal Research. Harvard University Press. Cambridge, Mass.
14. LINDSAY, R. B. 1963. The Role of Science in Civilization. Harper and Row. New York, N.Y.
15. ORLANS, H., ED. 1968. Science Policy and the University. The Brookings Institution. Washington, D.C.
16. PRICE, D. J. DES. 1963. Little Science, Big Science. Columbia University Press. New York, N.Y.
17. SHANNON, J. A. 1973. Science and the Evolution of Public Policy. The Rockefeller University Press. New York, N.Y.
18. TOBEY, R. C. 1971. The American Ideology of National Science. Pittsburgh University Press. Pittsburgh, Pa.
19. VAN TASSEL, D. B. & M. G. HALL. 1966. Science and Society in the United States. Dorsey Press. Homewood, Ill.
20. WIESNER, J. B. 1965. Where Science and Politics Meet. McGraw-Hill. New York, N.Y.
21. Biomedical Science and Its Administration (Woolridge Report). 1965. Report to the President. White House. Washington, D.C.
22. LEIGH, R. D. 1927. Federal Health Administration in the United States. Harper & Bros. New York, N.Y.
23. STRICKLAND, S. P. 1972. Politics, Science and Dread Disease. Harvard University Press. Cambridge, Mass.
24. Science and Technology in Presidential Policymaking: A Proposal. 1974. National Academy of Sciences. Washington, D.C.

Discussion

DR. SIEKEVITZ: When you first cited your hypothetical case, what came to my mind was the March of Dimes. Here was a private organization that was set up by relatively few people and that funneled a large amount of private funds into one area of research on a disease that afflicts actually a very small number of children in this country. Polio is not and was never a major disease. In this specific example is the public interest served better by having this pluralistic set-up? Or is it better served by a sort of elitist hierarchical administration that would more fairly and intelligently direct the funds?

DR. SHERMAN: This question involving private organizations such as the March of Dimes is always going to come up, for there are many examples of this sort of thing. I would reject that the alternative you suggested is the only choice. I strongly believe, given our pragmatic society and the contributions that an affluent nation can make to the public good through science and technology, that the better course lies somewhere in between and that the various inputs that result from a multiplicity of institutions help to shape the processes that serve public good, although admittedly in an inefficient and imprecise fashion.

To take the "polio" proposition as an example: If there had been an all-wise federal government directing the allocation of funds, the money would undoubtedly have been spent in improving the efficiency of the iron lung rather than in developing a vaccine. Furthermore, it seems to me that the whole area of virology was reborn as a consequence of the polio problem. Eventually not only the March of Dimes, but also the federal government and pharmaceutical firms joined forces in the development of that vaccine. So a very imprecise, inefficient system can serve our particular culture and country.

MR. DECKER: It seems to me that a fundamental argument has been brought to light by the first two speakers. I think this is the argument between a disjointed, incremental, remedial approach to science policy or policy-making in general, which Dr. Sherman has attempted to defend; and a coordinated, systematic, anticipatory approach to policy-making, which Dr. Fruchtbaum attempted to support. The question you have to ask in comparing these two is: What are the social trends that are emerging today that would make one approach better than the other? And the two factors that are brought up the most often are: more rapid social change and greater complexity. It is not clear, though, which approach those factors argue for. Those who support the systematic approach would claim that since there is more rapid social change, policy-makers have less lead-time and must think ahead and react more quickly, and that therefore they need a framework. And since society is more complex, they need a more systematic and coordinated approach to policy-making. Making one incremental change isn't going to have much effect.

On the other hand, the rapid social change and complexity of society make it much harder to have a systematic approach. We can't predict the future and we can't predict all the interrelationships that will occur. This then argues for a fragmented, incremental approach.

Another subissue to this is: To what extent does a systematic approach imply a centralized approach? I think that Dr. Sherman assumes that they are very closely correlated. I think that the Roses in their introductory presentation were making the assumption that you could have a systematic and pluralistic approach at the same time.

DR. E. MAUSS (*New York University, New York, N.Y.*): When Dr. Sherman and Dr. Fruchtbaum discuss the confrontation between two different points of view, I would hope there will be another hypothetical story that would tell us what would happen if that arresting question Dr. Fruchtbaum quoted at the end of his presentation were dealt with in any concrete way. It might grind this conference to a halt if we tried to really answer it. If the question of public policy were confronted so that the question of science policy could be put in its proper place, where would that take us in terms of the balance in this pluralistic approach?

J. SELZNICK: I was somewhat bemused by the speakers' reference to the present state of affairs as *pluralistic;* it's a term that gets thrown around a lot these days. For most people the term really signifies *dualistic,* and the models that usually come to mind are the two-party political system contending within itself, or the legal model where you have a plaintiff and a defendant, and their attorneys go at each other hammer and tongs and presumably the result is some equitable balance between them. From that point of view, is the present arrangement in the arriving-at of scientific policy really sufficiently dualistic? Is there enough representation and enough of an opposite point of view? I get the feeling that it's all very much *pro-*science people who are involved. It's much more like the kind of debate that might go on among defense attorneys about what should be the best strategy for their client; or a committee at a national convention determining what the party plank should be, rather than the really head-to-head confrontation that's supposed to arrive at an equitable middle ground. Is there sufficient representation from the nonscientific community? Is the question asked, for example, whether funds requested for a particular science project might not be socially better applied to some other nonscientific endeavor? And is it the scientific community's own responsibility to bring into this debate some representation from other points of view?

DR. SHERMAN: I would hark back to a comment made by the Roses last night: we have to remember to distinguish between strategy and tactics from time to time. Many of the things that I discussed in that hypothetical situation obviously were tactical in nature. But where the whole thing becomes a bit more complicated, it seems to me, is the fact that the process as it presently works doesn't distinguish between strategy and tactics. There is not a sufficiently clearly defined position, either by virtue of some policy or by legal or political precedents, to draw a good analogy between, for example, the two-party political system or the plaintiff-defendant relationship in a court of law. Rather, even within the government, to say nothing of the private sector, there is such a diversity of opinion and sometimes competition, as to make that analogy less useful. And so I would still opt for the pluralistic rather than the dualistic characterization. I also admit that were it possible to find some rational basis in national policy for guidelines to determine national science policy, we then ought to be able to approach the allocation of resources at the national level, and regardless of the source, in a fashion that would better serve the public interest, even over the short haul. This is not exactly the case at present, but I don't think it's that bad. Fortunately, to date our country has been sufficiently affluent so that we probably wasted less money in some of these areas than we have in others. But as the crunch comes, the scientific community should at least admit, if not encourage, practitioners in other areas to join in the development of policies as they affect the scientific enterprise. I'm not so certain that it isn't going to happen anyway. The lawyers have certainly moved in in great fashion. I think Seymour Melman, who will probably speak on this later, will give some assurance that the nature of the pluralistic process may become even more effective in the future. I also admit, as a former practicing scientist in the biomedical area, some trepidation as to that degree of involvement.

DR. J. H. MEYER *(E. R. Squibb & Sons, Inc. Princeton, N.J.)*: It seems to me that any science policy would have to address itself much more to strategy, if you can dichotomize between strategy and tactics. I wonder if Dr. Fruchtbaum, especially, would comment as to whether he thinks it's at all possible to establish a priori the reaction to these determinants as they happen dynamically in time. Can we sit back and take a forward-looking policy on how we're going to deal with yet-"unhappened" political, economic, and social interactions?

The other comment that I have is this: It seems to me that both speakers have looked at the issue primarily from a domestic American point of view. I feel that this is somewhat restrictive. Either way we tilt our approach to the issue; and we are certainly sitting in a shrinking world. I would like the speakers to comment on how we fit into today's and tomorrow's world.

[Dr. Fruchtbaum elected to answer these questions after the next paper.]

SCIENCE AND GOVERNMENT: PARTNERS IN SCIENCE PUBLIC POLICY

Howard J. Lewis

Office of Information
National Academy of Sciences
Washington, D.C. 20148

As a last-minute substitute I can afford to begin my remarks with a little candor. First of all, although I work at the National Academy of Sciences, I'm not a scientist. Second, although I edit a newsletter called *Public Science*, about science and public policy, I'm not a scholar of science and public policy.

Finally, I feel I owe an apology to those of you who paid in advance for not being Dan Greenberg. I'll do the best I can to be irreverent, but working as I do on the first floor of the "temple of science," or, as Dan calls it, "the established church of science," that takes some effort.

While I'm on the subject of my association with the National Academy of Sciences or, as we call it in Washington, "*The* Academy," I hope that all these earnest protestations of incompetence will make it unnecessary for me to announce that I'm not here to speak on behalf of the Academy or to represent its views in any way. It's possible that our views may accidentally coincide on occasion, but it should be understood that I'm speaking as a solitary observer at the interface of science and public policy. And I have the same social function, perhaps, as the amateur naturalists of the eighteenth and nineteenth centuries. Although what follows are some of my arboreal observations, you will have to look to others for data, analysis, and documentation. What I will provide is a personally conducted tour of the world I live in.

Let me begin by reciting the old Washington adage that where a man stands often depends on where he sits. And to that I'd like to add a corollary: that where a man stands determines what he will see. What has astonished me in my time in Washington and what continues to astonish me is how different are the worlds and perceptions of the scientists who would advise the government and the government officials they seek to advise. The differences are most broad in the dealings between the scientific community and the Congress, but only slightly less so in dealing with the executive agencies. It's almost as if they occupied different planets. And perhaps the most serious need is for a common language to make possible interplanetary communication.

Sometimes a problem arises from the different ways that intellectuals in general and responsible officials perceive real-time problems. In his new book, *The American Intellectual Elite*, Charles Kadushin quotes Norman Podhoretz at some length. Podhoretz told Kadushin of a trip to Washington to talk with "a high official" of the Kennedy adminstration who wanted to hear Podhoretz's ideas about a situation in Harlem:

> I had, as it happened, a great many of what I would have called ideas, and interesting ones, I thought, on this subject. But I noticed, while expounding them over a very good lunch, that the great man was growing restless and bored. This puzzled me, for I thought I was speaking well. Faltering a bit in response to his impatience, I asked him whether he disagreed with what I

was saying. 'No, no,' he answered. 'What you're saying is all very well, but what should we do about it?' 'Do?' I was not accustomed to thinking in such terms. I was accustomed to making critical analyses whose point was to understand a problem as fully as possible, not to affect or manipulate it.

The insights shown in this fragment have a familiar ring to those of us who have witnessed the too frequent mismatches of impedance between the scientific community and the government. To the scientist, simply acquiring an understanding of the problem is half or more of the battle. To the politician, it may mean a wasted afternoon. In some respects, one might say that the scientist and politician are separated by a common problem. The politician has a question concerning some large national policy issue with a major component of science or technology. He needs help either because the most desirable scientific solution has political drawbacks, or the desirable political solution has scientific problems associated with it. It is vitally important at this point to recognize that scientific and political factors are virtually inextricable.

For years a number of individuals have proposed that some kind of an institution be established into which the nation could feed these complex problems, and then by some masterful process, this new institution would then separate all the scientific and technical questions from the political ones, solve the former and return the issues back to the nation so that the political components of these problems might now be amicably settled in the proper forums. However, I feel obligated to point out that although it is not difficult to describe and to separate these issues in such a fashion, it is just shadow-boxing. As Howard Margolis and others have pointed out, in political government, the framing of the question often determines the nature of the answer.

In effect, then, the politician has something of a cost-benefit problem facing him in which technical considerations play a substantial role. But the scientist also has a cost-benefit problem facing him. How can he provide advice that is politically useful without paying too much of a cost among his own peer group? The scientist would prefer to wait until there were sufficient data on which to base an answer. Even then, he insists upon all the standard qualifications to protect himself against peer-group criticism. But political leaders can't wait until all the data are in. They need an answer by next Tuesday, because that is when the bill is going to be on the floor. And error bars will drive a politician or congressman right up the wall.

My personal vantage point makes me optimistic. There is no question that a number of major political issues involving large questions of science and technology grow monthly. There is actually now some serious concern that if adequate scientific input was made to all the newly developing questions at the level required, we may quickly find ourselves suffering from a genuine shortage of competent people. It is my understanding that there are already a number of narrow technical areas where it is difficult to find new people with the necessary competence and judgment, who have not already taken public positions on the basis of their prior evaluation of the available data.

My optimism, however, grows out of the fact that I see an increasing sophistication on the part of the scientific community with regard to the nature of the advisory role and its inherent difficulties and limitations. But we have a long way to go on both sides. I have long felt that the government knows a lot more about science than the scientific community knows about government. When it comes to understanding how each other approaches a policy problem, however, both sectors seem to be equally innocent. Yet they're beginning to learn. I was especially heartened by the interaction between the N.A.S. Commission on Natural Resources and the Senate Committee on Public Works with regard to statutory limitations on motor vehicle emissions. The Academy testimony included an appreciation of the need to establish standards before there were adequate supporting data. The Senate Committee appeared to understand why it was impossible to make unequivocal statements on the basis of the data available.

Let me suggest a typical scenario for the generation of the treatment of a problem in science and public policy. A unit within the government wishes to start a project or to block one that some other group wants to start. The ultimate question of public benefits and costs involves scientific considerations. Now, that unit of the government that expects the scientific community to support its position will contract with a research institution for a study of the question. If the unit desiring the study is a committee of the Congress, it can seek approval to get a contract as did the Senate Committee on Public Works; or it can, through the appropriations mechanism, mandate such a study to be supported by a willing or unwilling federal agency.

The question that is posed to the scientific body is customarily framed in such a way as to maximize the likelihood of a favorable answer. But it is also obvious from the language that the scientific group is being asked to answer a basically political question. If it chooses to accept the question in this form, it runs the risk that the final report will simply summarize the political judgments or biases, not the scientific judgments of the study group. It is more likely that the study group will reformulate the question so that it sounds more like a scientific question. It's also likely that the dimensions of the question will be changed somewhat to conform to the tastes of the chairman. Is he a holist? He will want to enlarge the question so that the entire system is under study. "Our response will have no meaning unless we examine the entire system."

On the other hand, the chairman may be more of a traditionalist. He will massage the question, snipping a bit here or there until it looks like a study that is doable. He says, "No point in tackling a question unless there is a reasonable likelihood that a scientifically defensible answer can be found." In any event, the question that is now being explored may be considerably different from the one that originally concerned the government sponsors.

The all-too-frequent result of all this manipulating of the question is that the report that goes to the sponsoring agency will not be satisfactory. It may be very good science, yet vaguely disappointing to the sponsor—like a slice of prime roast beef when one expects a steak. And if that is the case, it will probably be even more disappointing to the study group because it is likely that the report will have little influence on policymaking.

I trust that it is not necessary to point out that there are many exceptions to this scenario, more than enough to increase the budget of the National Academy by 10 percent a year in constant dollars, with most of it going to policy studies of one kind or another. But from where I sit, I see a great need for the development of a new kind of administrator, one who is able to appreciate both the needs of the sociopolitical community for a useful study and the requirements of the scientific and technical community for an acceptable professional context in which the study can be carried out.

Before climbing down from this podium, I want to get something off my chest. I would like to propose a moratorium on the pronouncement that the United

States doesn't have a national science policy. That's a cliché. I've used it myself. The group from the Organization for Economic Cooperation and Development, which examined science in the United States some years back, said it. But I submit that we do have a national science policy to the same exent that we have a national defense policy, a national economic policy, or a national foreign policy. There are several elements to it. One is that the federal government appreciates the social, economic, and political benefits of a vigorous program of research and development, and willingly assumes a major portion of the responsibility for its support, especially with regard to fundamental research. Furthermore, the government has decided that there shall be plural sources of support, more centralized with regard to the support of fundamental research and less centralized with regard to the support of applied research. The mission agencies are expected to support those areas of pure and applied research most clearly closely related to that mission. An element that is missing is a responsibility on the part of the federal government to look ahead in the planning for the production of scientific manpower.

However, it would appear to me that these statements constitute an effective national science policy. I'm not sure that a national foreign policy could be stated with equal simplicity or equal exactness.

Discussion

Mr. C. Decker (*Office of Technology Assessment, Washington, D.C.*) I speak for myself here and not for the OTA. I would like to focus on the difference between technology evaluation and technology assessment, and in doing so, try to integrate some of the ideas that the Roses have presented with those of Dr. Fruchtbaum and others we have just heard. This is important because to an extent these are both *macro* and *micro* approaches to the same kind of issues.

And the way I'd like to do this is to focus on some of the unfoldings of OTA. Although it is too early for a complete assessment—OTA has only been operating for less than a year—we can make some generalizations about its opening months.

I believe that the OTA was the response to many of the concerns that the Roses have already expressed. Either a political or an historical explanation can be offered for the creation of OTA. Politically, you might say that Senator Kennedy's active interest is what got it through. Or you might say that the bill for its creation was passed because of the dislike by many congressmen of Nixon's policies of impoundment and withholding information from Congress. Of course, that goes back to the knowledge-as-commodity paradigm that the Roses cited yesterday, so this is also an historical explanation. Other historical explanations for the development of the OTA include the new pervasiveness of science and technology in society; the sense of momentum behind technology and a loss of control over it. Boorstin, in his latest book, *The Democratic Experience* noted that among American citizens there has been a shift from a feeling of mission to one of helplessness in the face of a momentum over which they have little control, and which has been mostly brought about by large technical projects like the splitting of the atom and the space program. Other historical causes were the ecological and the consumer movements; the antiwar movement; the questioning of the military-industrial complex; the antitechnology and counterculture philosophers, including Ellul, Marcuse, Mumford, and Roszak; and the limits-of-growth debate.

All of these historical reasons contributed to the original conception of the OTA as an early warning system and a watchdog on the negative aspects of technology. The OTA was also viewed as a way of integrating different technical and social areas and as a systems approach to policy formulation.

I agree with Mr. Lewis that, at least in the short-term, the concept of technology assessment has shifted away from that of looking at indirect social impacts and long-term integration of policy towards one of shorter term technology evaluation and technology feasibility. I'd like to examine a few of the institutional factors and reasons contributing to this shift.

First, several factors combined to make it very important that the OTA appear very responsive to Congress in its first few years of operations. These include suspicion among conservatives about Kennedy's motives in setting up the OTA; the decision to make the board of directors for the OTA an all-congressional board with six senators and six representatives, which then made it look like a joint committee, causing some concern among other committees about infringement on their authority or areas; and then, some resistance by the administration and, at the same time, the dissolution of the OST. Therefore, it was very important for the OTA to appear to be very responsive to congressional needs.

Congressman have greater concern with the short-term and feasibility questions than with the long-term questions of far-reaching social impact. This is particularly true of the present social climate. The energy crisis has caused a lot of people to be more concerned about developing the technology to obtain energy rather than considering the environmental or social consequences of that technology. Furthermore, the term, technology assessment, is misleading. To many congressmen what that means is looking at technology feasibility. Perhaps a better term would have been social-impact analysis. But, as people have argued, if it had been called social-impact analysis, the bill probably never would have been passed. A third point is something that Daniel Greenberg has formalized in his second law, which is: don't ask a barber if you need a haircut. Scientists are the worst people to ask about whether or not a technology should be developed, because their economic interests are in developing that technology.

There is some hope, however, and I'd like to add some laws to Dan Greenberg's, based on my experience with barbers. One of the things I've noticed is that barbers tend to cut your hair very short, which seems to be connected with their values or attitudes or perceptions, even though it's in opposition to their economic interests. In the same way, scientists have the myth or the value of nonpartisanism or objectivity, which, of course, is a folly to a certain extent. At the same time it presents an opportunity or a hope that scientists will not always behave in their economic interest, but will throw their support behind the larger public interest. The final law that I would propose is that, although barbers initially cut the hair too short, they have been able to adapt to a behavior that's more fitting to their economic interests. They've changed their values and now they cut hair longer, and also they charge you more for it by calling it hair-styling rather than a haircut. Similarly there is the danger that scientists will set aside their values of objectivity when it's in their best interests. And so, the interplay between the last two laws I proposed is something that has to be considered carefully.

The movement toward technology feasibility in and out of the OTA may not necessarily negate the original goals of technology assessment. In fact, it may instead lead to a wider definition of what technology feasibility is: For technology to be feasible, not only must the primary technology be economically and technically feasible, but also there must be provision for technical or social correctives for whatever negative secondary side-effects may accrue from the primary technology.

Let me give some examples: Data bases that cannot insure personal privacy under this new wider definition would not be technically feasible. A lot of investigators are trying to look for technical fixes for the problem of insuring the privacy and security of data. There is another example, which is probably further off: Nuclear power would not be considered technically feasible if it leads to greater centralization and concentration of power by the rich. Under such an assumption, nuclear power might not be considered technically feasible, but solar energy, which leads to greater decentralization, might be considered to be more technically feasible, even though it is not economically as cheap as nuclear power.

DR. FRUCHTBAUM: Several issues were raised that I will try to address.

My difficulty in responding is due to the fact that my view of what are the global and the national realities is significantly different, I think, from the views expressed by my colleagues on the panel and members of the audience. At the risk of outraging a number of you, let me talk about my own sense of present day realities, because in doing so I will be able to address myself to Dr. Meyer's question concerning national science policy from a world perspective.

When I wrote my paper, focusing on the historical development of science policy in this country, I was painfully aware of the global situation, which is critical for that policy. Let me put it directly and cut to the heart of the matter. It is simply this: the United States is the major counterrevolutionary force in the world today. Science and technology are used in maintaining its position through economic penetration, military and police support, counterinsurgency, intelligence data collection, and so forth. This means that American policies for science and technology are shaped in a very particular way. Who makes these policies, and how are they implemented and whose interests are served? If we are to really understand what is happening in this country and elsewhere, we must answer questions of this sort.

As far as I am able to see, fascism is on the rise; the list of countries that might be so characterized is quite long. That gives me additional cause for pessimism. On the other hand, there are important and encouraging developments in Greece and Portugal and in a number of other countries. What is happening among young people and workers gives cause for hope that there will be more and more participation in democratic movements.

In this country, there is reason for pessimism, given our domestic and foreign policies. On the other hand, I think there is also cause for some optimism in a number of democratic people's movements. We see this in health care, where people are demanding a role in decision-making and are becoming very much concerned with ethical questions. But as the economic situation deteriorates and capitalism sinks deeper into difficulty, as I think it will, the pressures in this country are going to grow. There's a real danger that this society will move not to the left but sharply to the right, and technology used to maintain totalitarian control.

My concern, therefore, is how to stimulate democratic forms at all levels of society. How does one involve the people in decision-making so that our policies abroad and at home serve humane and democratic ends? Unless we work out answers to these questions and provide the appropriate social and political mechanisms that will be responsive to the needs of people and the requirements of social justice, our future is indeed grim.

A coordinated national science policy could be implemented through a decentralized system electronically tied together. The process of policy formulation, evaluation and adjustment would be continual as well as sensitive to the information flowing through the network, so that local and regional needs and capabilities would influence national policies. I have no difficulty envisioning a decentralized system. The problem is how to create such a system so that people throughout the society are brought into decision-making.

In discussions of this kind, especially when opinions are very different, we face the problem of talking past one another. What I have been saying may not be relevant to current technology assessment or related issues. But it is imperative that we do not go on talking about science policy as if it has nothing to do with what our government does at home and in other nations.

DR. SHERMAN: I couldn't agree more with Dr. Fruchtbaum's concerns about the need to expand the base, both in terms of numbers and variety of inputs, in the development of what we refer to as national science policy. I agree with Howard Lewis on this point. The concern I have is the same that he obviously shares, namely, that the big issue is not the "what" but the "how." I would suggest picking up on the remark made by Elizabeth Barrett last night that biomedical research may offer more possibilities for analysis, if not for implementation, of how we, as a nation, and as individuals caught between this array of public and private institutions, might go about that process. On the basis of experience with biomedical research, I disagree with Dr. Fruchtbaum's pessimism with respect to science and its contributions. For example: one of the most productive, but little-known international exercises of recent years in biomedical research was that initiated by President Johnson and then-President Sato of Japan. There was established a continuous exchange of scientific personnel and particularly of information in about a half a dozen different areas of common interest to Japan and this country. This program was initially under the auspices of the State Department, but was quickly delegated to the scientific community. The success of that program can be attributed to the fact that very quickly politicians constructed an overall framework and then, for whatever reason, either got out or were forced out of the act, with the result that ever since then, it has been in the hands of working scientists. If one reviews that program, and I don't think the Congress has taken any particular interest in it, one can see an opportunity to develop in microcosm a very useful international exchange related both to policy and to specific activities in the scientific area.

Addressing myself to Craig Decker's comment about the basic issue here being the fragmented approach to a systematic problem, I couldn't agree more with the attractiveness of Dr. Fruchtbaum's concept, nor disagree more with the possibility for its adoption in the foreseeable future. The pluralistic nature of our society as well as that of other countries makes me quite pessimistic about the practicality of relying too much on that. I would urge the Roses and the Fruchtbaums of this world to continue their quest, but I would expect that they would not be very successful in terms of implementation in the foreseeable future in this country.

Lastly, I agree that we must concern ourselves about this matter of protection, given the threat of moves to the political right throughout the world. It represents an area where science and technology are probably most vulnerable in terms of its application. However, I am a believer in either the rhythm system of society or the extremes of the pendulum swings, and I expect that we are now in one of those periods where science and technology have more to contribute, but paradoxically we have more to fear from them.

MR. LEWIS: I'm a little abashed at tackling a question like this because I consider myself more of a reporter than a philosopher. And philosophers have the benefit of first trying out their ideas on their friends, and dismissing the ideas that sound silly. So I'll have to try them all out on you.

With regard to the large question that was posed that some people—and sometimes pathologically—like power more than other people, I would reply that one way to get power is through governance. The persons with control in government have power, and then seek other systems that permit them to enlarge the scope of power. In recent years, science and technology, as a system, has enabled ruling classes to consolidate their power. So there is much to be listened to in what the Roses and Dr. Fruchtbaum had to say with regard to the role of the scientific worker in that system.

Last night, as Dr. Rose was describing this system, I couldn't help but think that he was likening science to a Mexican jumping bean: the larva inside feels that he is the master of his domain, but he can't control whose pocket he's in.

Perhaps because optimism is a necessary condition for survival, I feel that, of all the countries I know, it is in this one that science and technology are most loosely under control. Secondly, of all institutions, science is the hardest to control and the most pluralistic in its governance. And I'm content to remember, when Dr. Fruchtbaum talks about how science is often used by the United States as a counterrevolutionary force in the world, that it's also being used at the National Academy of Sciences to show how to use ferrocement in building boats, how to deal with kwashiorkor, and for many other beneficial purposes. Maybe I'm just too old to be a revolutionary any more, but I find there's still a good life to be led in the ameliorative process.

UNIDENTIFIED SPEAKER: I don't want to politicize science, because too many things are being politicized. When we politicize science we get into the question of targeted science and forget about basic science. We must remember that although targeted science is very practical, you can't make progress in the future without basic background science. Problem-oriented science takes a "roll up your sleeves and solve the problem" approach. But most scientific advances have been made simply because we've nailed up the background of knowledge in general. A very good report has been made by the Illinois Institute of Technology on this very subject. They cited several scientific discoveries such as "the pill" and the computer, demonstrating how basic scientific discoveries in the past allowed these final products to result. For instance, Papanicolaou at Cornell was working on the physiology of reproduction. But the "pull-out" out of this research was the famous Pap test and the pill. These end-products could not have resulted without *un*applied research. As a result we have an attitude of "you worry about the government, and I'll worry about the medicine." Furthermore the solution to many problems is not susceptible to just pouring in a lot of money.

DR. SHERMAN: I agree totally, and would add one further comment. With reference to my observations on the biomedical area, one of the problems that worries me now is the degree of overeagerness on the part of the scientific community to adjust their views and their willingness to accept forms and levels of support which, as you have indicated, are predicated on a science base that is not strong.

For example: the Congress and the Executive Branch as well as the scientific community ought to look very carefully to what has happened to the concept of centers programs within the biomedical community—an understandable effort to bring together teams of scientists from a variety of disciplines to work on very well-agreed upon societal problems. The cancer program is a good example of this. Without being overcritical of it, I believe it represents an attraction for the political body that has not had enough debate in terms of its impact on the development of young scientists, their attitudes, their sometime-failure to recognize their limitations, scientifically and otherwise, as well as whether or not in comparison with the good, old research project grant, this is the best way to allocate that sum of money. This is not to argue the question of overall allocation, which is still another story.

MR. DECKER: I think that Dr. Fruchtbaum dealt rather simplistically with the question of centralization and coordination—whether you can have both at the same time. To take his example of the electronic networks, what the Roses were suggesting yesterday was that all technology is going to be used by the infrastructure to promote central control and centralization. The largest electronic network in this country, the ARPN-network, is controlled and completely funded by the Defense Department. There is truth in what Dr. Fruchtbaum says, but basically he's going back to the idea that technology is neutral. I believe that you can't separate the technology from the infrastructure that's driving it.

Dr. Sherman, it's true that it's more difficult today to have a systematic approach because of the complexity, but nevertheless the imperativeness of the problem overrides that objection. It is imperative because, as society gets more complex, you have positive feedback, that is, problems get worse all by themselves. Therefore if you wait to take remedial action, you pay an increasing price as the problem accelerates. Another problem is that of negative feedback loops, that institutions (or any incremental change) tend to reach the original equilibrium. So any disjointed or incremental change you make tends to have no effect on the system. Those are the two critical new dimensions of modern society that argue for a systematic approach.

PART II. FEDERAL AND NONPROFIT SECTOR INSTITUTIONS AND THEIR INFLUENCE ON SCIENCE PUBLIC POLICY

FOUNDATIONS AND SCIENCE PUBLIC POLICY

E. Creutz and Wayne R. Gruner

*National Science Foundation
Washington, D.C. 20550*

Introduction

The title of this paper employs several words that do not have unique, well-defined meanings. Moreover, we haven't discovered any powerful organizing principle for the ideas to be discussed. So I must apologize for any incorrect expectations that may have been aroused.

Consider the word "foundation." Is the Smithsonian Institution a "foundation," or a museum? Was the Office of Naval Research, when it supported research in molecular biology and high-energy physics, acting as a "foundation," or as part of the celebrated "military-industrial complex"? How about the Air Force Office of Scientific Research, when it supported work in gravitational theory and general relativity? What about the National Institutes of Health, when it awards career development grants to promising young scientists, or the AEC when it supports studies in high-energy physics? Are they acting as "foundations" or as "mission agencies"? One of the intriguing things about our federal government is that many of its agencies perform functions that don't seem to be implicit either in their names or in their statutory missions.

Then, too, different people focus their attention upon different sets of ideas when they hear the phrase "science public policy." To some, this means the manner of selection and promotion of applied science intended for use in specific predetermined contexts. Such people think of "science policy" in terms, for example, of those biological and clinical researches popularly termed the "war on cancer"; research conducted in support of our national controlled thermonuclear fusion effort; applied research intended to improve the technology by which coal is mined and used; and the like. One has several specific public objectives in mind, and the policy questions are: What relative weights and degrees of support ought to be attached to these different objectives? How ought the scientific and technical work be organized and managed to produce maximal effect?

Another group of people are more preoccupied with "technology assessment" and related notions. To them "science public policy" means the way in which analyses of the scientific background of various general public policy problems are initiated, organized, and carried through. This might include study of the economic and climatic consequences of the SST; or the long-term consequences of using large quantities of chemical pesticides and chemical fertilizers in agriculture; or the implications of heavy dependence upon private motor vehicles for transportation; or the influences upon world climate of continually increasing industrialization; and so on.

Finally, there is the set of preoccupations with which the National Science Foundation is most closely identified, and which I intend to discuss in greater detail, that is, policies for the promotion of science per se.

Of course these various conceptions of "science public policy" are linked in multiple ways, and are by no means independent or cleanly separable. But, despite their interdependence, I believe there is a serious question as to whether—at least in a system as pluralistic as ours—"national science policy" can ever be a real, taxonomically classifiable animal at all. Probably it's more of a unicorn or sphinx! Our "science policy," in any of the senses mentioned above, tends to be simply an uncritical assemblage of facets of other policies (e.g., public health policy, energy policy, welfare policy, etc.), many of which are not themselves very coherent and not very logically interrelated. To make either a successful policy, or a successful conspiracy, requires some considerable degree of control and discipline, more, perhaps, than is to be found in most complex democratic societies. I don't mean to suggest here that it's a "good thing" that various elements and parts of science policy are somewhat fragmented or scattered around but only to remark that it's a fact.

I suppose we all *dream* occasionally of a world where science policy would be deductively related to some set of generally understood and agreed-upon social goals, and administered by rational decision-makers who would optimize all the cost-benefit ratios, of course taking due account of intangible costs and benefits. But, as everyone here knows, the real world is too complicated for that. If you want to get just a hint of *how* complicated, and see a conscientious critique of the ends-means calculus, I might refer you to Laurence Tribe's article, "Policy science: Analysis or ideology?" in *Philosophy & Public Affairs* (Fall 1972, Vol. 2, Number 1).

Background

So I am not going to propose any grand themes. I am going to discuss primarily one organization, the National Science Foundation, with which I happen to be generally familiar—emphasizing policy *toward* science. But first I will try to provide a little bit in the way of historical context. If one reads A. Hunter Dupree's *Science and the Federal Government,* Raymond B. Fosdick's *The Story of the Rockefeller Foundation,* Abraham Flexner's *Funds and Foundations,* or *Science and Society in the United States* (edited by Van Tassel and Hall), he may notice first of all that the history of the United States' policy *toward* science has been dominated from the beginning mostly by utilitarian considerations. It has been concerned primarily with science for use—for use in agriculture, for use in medicine and public health, for use in aviation, for use in industry, and science for military applications. This is as true of private philanthropists and private foundations as it is of government.

Apart from this tendency toward utilitarian preoccupation (and, of course, endless wrangling in governmental quarters over expense) history seems to show that science usually has been accepted on its own terms by its patrons, both public and private. That is, one finds little evidence of sponsoring agencies or foundations attempting to specify either the method or the substantive content of scientific research once the *general* limits of areas to be explored were agreed upon. There is no evidence of Lysenko-type episodes. And the interpretation of science as "objective" has not been seriously questioned by its sponsors.

Another thing to note is that the present science support system in the United States, although heavily dominated by *government,* finds many, perhaps most, of its models and precedents in the initiatives of *private* individuals and foundations. The list includes fellowships, research grants, research institutes, university development grants, and large-scale public health programs. Specific examples include the Rockefeller Institute, the Carnegie Institution of Washington, the Social Science Research Council, the National Bureau of Economic Research, the Mt. Wilson Observatory and 100-inch telescope, the Mt. Palomar-Observatory and 200-inch telescope, the 184-inch Berkeley cyclotron, the Brookings Institution, the Woods Hole Laboratory, the Peking Union Medical College, the International Maize and Wheat Improvement Center, the Gunnar Myrdal study of negro sociology in the United States, and the Kinsey study. Notice that this list includes a great number of research-*performing* organizations which have later been relied upon for the conduct of government-sponsored work. Moreover, and this is much more important than generally realized, you see here that the private foundations established precedents for the *scale* on which scientific research might be, or must be, conducted in order to be effective. Thus, the list I just read you includes the two largest optical telescopes in use in the world until very recent times. Gunnar Myrdal's "American Dilemma" study was (with the exception of the United States Census) probably the most ambitious and largest piece of social science research ever to be conducted at its time, and it still remains one of the largest. The 184-inch cyclotron at Berkeley was the first major particle accelerator.

Probably the most striking thing to be observed is the extraordinary overall results and, to use a trite phrase, "cost-effectiveness," of the efforts of the great private foundations in the first half of this century. With expenditures that would seem trivial by today's standards, organizations like Carnegie and Rockefeller brought about vast sweeping changes in education, public health, medicine, and a great strengthening of scientific research. Up to 1950, for example, Rockefeller had spent about $30 million in support of basic biological research and a roughly comparable sum on basic social science. It seems that the present world population problem may be in good part a result of the expenditure by one or two great private foundations of a couple of hundred million dollars. That's a fraction of one year's current obligational authority for federally sponsored *basic* research alone.

Now what could have accounted for this impressive cost-effectiveness of the scientific and technical activities sponsored by private foundations in the first half of the century? It remains impressive even after one has fully discounted not only the monetary inflation that occurred since that time, but also the fact that the support was *enabling* assistance and that questions of "full overhead" or "indirect costs" did not arise. One may speculate on several characteristics.

Private foundation efforts were mostly concentrated on quite specific targets. They were not "across-the-board" efforts to support and sustain entire fields of science or technology. They were generally directed to badly neglected areas, that is, to problems that had not previously received high quality and well-organized intellectual attention. So *historical opportunity* was an important ingredient.

The approach of the private foundations, whether it was to selection of recipients for fellowships and research grants or to finding the leaders for public health projects, was thoroughly elitist. Every effort was made to find the few most promising individuals and to gamble on talent.

The private foundations mounted few, if any, "crash" programs as the phrase is understood today. The emphasis was on sound method and promising ideas, not on deadlines and timetables. There was little or no advance fanfare. Indeed, none was required since it was a time of relatively modest expectations, and the rhetoric that goes, "If we can land a man on the moon, then why can't we—" had not yet been invented. There was a minimum of other complications. International programs, for example, were fairly devoid of politics, of whatever sign, and very few, if any, interventions were undertaken with overt redistributionist intent.

So, when the federal government, in the period immediately following the Second World War, began to support science on a large scale, there existed—in addition to the war-time OSRD, Manhattan Project, and Radiation Lab experience—a great deal of experience that had accumulated in the first half of the century from the activities of the private foundations. In particular, there were precedents for the establishment of large scientific facilities, research-performing institutes or centers, and organized programs in a wide range of scientific fields. Some of the leading personalities (for example, Warren Weaver and Vannevar Bush) who campaigned for establishment of a National Science Foundation and who shaped its initial policies and those of its predecessor and prototype organization, ONR, were experienced in the operations of the private foundations.

Having provided this much by way of background, let me summarize by saying that the successes of the private foundations and of the wartime federal programs provided models and precedents, and, as the saying goes, were "a hard act to follow." Expectations had been raised very high.

The National Science Foundation

Now I will try to give you some idea of the National Science Foundation's approach to the fostering of science per se. Although, as I have indicated above, it would be an oversimplification to ask about a global "national policy for science," it is still fair to say that public support of scientific research, specifically including *basic* research, is now a generally accepted *ingredient* of federal policies. Such support has two recognized major objectives: (1) To foster and maintain basic research as an investment toward future opportunities, as insurance against unforeseeable future dangers, and as a vital element of culture. (2) To bring about prompt, effective performance of applied research and problem-oriented basic research insofar as specific needs for these can be foreseen in the light of current understanding.

It is not possible to make the distinction between basic and applied research a sharp one, and the National Science Foundation is *one of several* federal agencies that support research of *both* kinds. The Foundation, however, is unique in its mission to foster basic research per se and in its responsibility for *future* scientific research capability. Unlike private foundations or mission agencies, the NSF has an across-the-board responsibility for the health of science. It may pick targets for special attention, but it has no charter to disregard or ignore any intellectually legitimate segment of science. Since the Foundation, as I have said, has responsibility for the future scientific research capability or potential of the nation, its freedom to make purely "seed money" type interventions is very limited. That is, the Foundation must sustain as well as initiate. We must balance the *continuation* of science with the initiation of totally *new* endeavors.

It is very important to maintain the interest and the morale of the scientific community in the face of fluctuations of the political climate for its support. The importance of this, perhaps, has not been sufficiently appreciated until very recently. But one can very well argue that it is more important to society to possess a sustained high-quality scientific capability over the long pull than it is to make a string of exciting discoveries in the immediate future, possibly excepting certain particular areas of oriented research. I take it, therefore, that NSF's major unique responsibility is not only to the overall health of science, of basic science in particular, but also to the long-term maintenance of this health. In my Congressional testimony a year and a half ago I emphasized that: "... continuity of the human capability may be the most vital thing we ensure to the future by our present investment in scientific research."

The public accountability of the National Science Foundation is also of a different kind from that of the private foundations. Although the latter must refrain from certain kinds of activities that might be so politically objectionable as to alter their special tax status and public charter, they are under no obligation to please all, or even most, of the people all or most of the time. The National Science Foundation, on the other hand, must convince the OMB and the Congress each year that the impact of all of its programs amounts to a positive good commensurate with the cost and that it has dealt in a fair and equitable manner with all of its actual and potential clientele. The question of comparative efficiency at the margin is with us at every moment.

Now, what kind of considerations do these peculiarities of our situation thrust upon us? One is the division of labor with the mission agencies. The Foundation, as I have pointed out, is only one of several federal agencies that support basic research. The established and constantly reaffirmed policy of the Executive Office is that the mission agencies shall conduct not only applied research but also that basic research which is germane to their missions. However, this leaves open a big question: Exactly how is the notion "mission-related" to be interpreted? Concerning the answer to this, honest men may experience serious disagreement, originating primarily from differences in time-horizon, imaginative style, and tolerance of ambiguity.

One must not be surprised, therefore, in dealing with any large mission agency, especially one as complex as the Department of Defense, to find within it numerous influential individuals with a very diverse range of opinions as to what kinds of basic research qualify as mission-related. These individuals and their differing interpretations are constantly vying with one another in what might be called a "policy market." And when interpretations shift, the "health of science" is affected and the reverberations are felt in the National Science Foundation.

From time to time, in fact, some external event or influence, for example the Mansfield Amendment, *does* shift the weight of influence within the mission agencies from one faction to another, and allocation patterns change. This sort of process, of course, goes on not only in the Defense Department but in other large mission agencies as well. Interestingly, the Mansfield Amendment was enacted at a time when public affairs generally were characterized by a great crescendo in the "rhetoric of relevance." And, as the Department of Defense moved toward "strict construction" of mission-relatedness under Mansfield's prodding, somewhat similar programming shifts occurred in several other agencies (e.g., NIH), without any suggestion of statutory compulsion. *Each* such shift requires reappraisal by NSF of the overall national balance of effort.

The allocation process is unavoidably hierarchical. The levels of the hierarchy correspond to levels of aggregation of scientific disciplines. Thus at the highest level, allocations are made to the physical sciences, the biological sciences, the social sciences, etc. At the next lower level, allocations are specified to entire disciplines such as physics, chemistry, astronomy, sociology, economics, and anthropology. At the next lower level, allocation is made to the usually recognized sub-disciplines like solid-state physics or enzyme chemistry. Finally, the last step of the allocation process is the selection of individual research projects within the sub-disciplines.

High-level allocations to disciplines and groups of disciplines unavoidably require judgments, which must be formulated in a context where consensus is impossible. We know of no universally accepted standard or principle that can be applied either to perform this allocation process or to judge the result. Federal administrators are forced simply to do the best they can in the light of scientific, social, economic, and political information available to them and to watch very closely for signs of error, so that within a reasonable time corrections can be made. Our sources of information are numerous and diverse. They include: the National Science Board; several high-level NSF advisory committees; more than 25 disciplinary advisory panels; studies performed by the National Academy of Sciences; inputs from professional societies; the views expressed by our authorization and appropriations committees in both houses of Congress; guidance from the Office of Management and Budget; information received from administrators in other Federal agencies; and a great deal of unsolicited correspondence from members of the scientific community and the general public. This kind of broad participatory planning is something quite foreign, I believe, to the operation of private foundations.

Inevitably, the distribution of support among fields of science represents a difficult balancing between what we consider the *desirability* and relative importance of scientific progress in particular areas and our best judgment of the *attainability* of that progress with given resources. Attainability, of course, depends upon the quality and power of the scientific ideas available at the moment, upon the insight and ingenuity of participating scientists, and upon the experimental facilities and methods that are at hand or that scientists know how to construct. This problem is well known to the private foundations. In 1939, for example, we find J. H. Willits saying to the Rockefeller Foundation trustees (concerning social sciences): "All proposals should be scanned most severely, as the obvious danger is that the depth of our desire to aid may so easily lead to doing things that are futile and are endorsed only by their fine hopes."

Even a program of basic research may properly use criteria of anticipated social utility to help shape its allocational pattern. Here, as is true to some degree even for applied research, we judge it most productive to apply these "relevance" criteria not on a project-by-project basis but rather to entire *fields* of science or areas of investigation. We are very keenly aware of the difficulty of making such judgments, especially the negative ones (that is, conclusions that a certain field is not "relevant"), with any degree of confidence. History seems to show that sooner or later the "best" science (by the criteria of intrinsic merit) almost invariably turns out to be the most useful—often in totally unforeseeable applied contexts. Once the general emphasis is decided upon, we believe it best to use criteria of intrinsic scientific merit in the allocation to specific individual projects.

And as one gets down to the level of subdisciplinary programs and individual projects, consensus is easier to develop, and peer judgment becomes an effective tool for allocation. The mechanics of peer evaluation in its different forms are too well known to require detailed discussion in this paper.* What may not be sufficiently recognized is the very great breadth of participation by members of the scientific community in this peer evaluation process. In evaluating the current year's accession of scientific research project proposals, for example, the National Science Foundation will obtain the opinions of more than 18,000 different scientists. These are scientists from universities, from government laboratories, from industrial laboratories, and from nonprofit research organizations. Some are retired and some, in special cases, are foreign citizens. In all cases the reviewers are

---

* Fuller discussion may be found in testimony of Dr. Edward Creutz, Assistant Director for Research, 1974 National Science Foundation Authorization Hearings before the Subcommittee on Science, Research, and Development of the Committee of Science and Astronautics, U.S. House of Representatives, Ninety-third Congress, First Session: 63–149. U.S. Government Printing Office, Washington, D.C., 1973.

chosen for their special knowledge of the field of science, of the investigator, of the institutional environment where the work will be carried out, or of combinations of these factors. The advice of these reviewers is further augmented by that of advisory panels. I believe this kind of *institutionalized* peer evaluation was never elaborately developed by the private foundations.

A different dimension—and one in which confident judgment or consensus is again hard to attain—has to do with the concentration of support in a smaller number of major efforts as against its widespread distribution to a large number of smaller projects. For any given overall science budget, there is obviously a reciprocal relationship between what one might call the average "unit cost" of supporting a scientist or a scientific project and the number of scientists or projects that can be supported. Federal administrators must be concerned with more than the accumulation of scientific knowledge. They must consider also the state of living knowledge; that is, scientific "know-how" in the minds and hands of people who are practiced and skilled at working with it and applying it. Widespread participation in the scientific enterprise is an important element of national well-being, and we must be apprehensive of reductions in the number of participants or unnecessary curtailment of their distribution throughout our nation. This, of course, is a consideration which need not unduly concern a private foundation.

On the other hand, scientific research depends increasingly upon technology (just as technology depends upon science). In consequence of its own progress, scientific research each year becomes more exacting; the unsolved problems, on the average, become more subtle, difficult, and complex, and the methods and equipment necessary for further progress tend to grow more sophisticated and expensive. In short, the technology required to support science grows in costliness, and the "unit cost" of really first-rate science increases.

Thus, we are often faced with the very hard choice of either restraining breadth of participation in science or maintaining participation at the cost of letting the technology of science become static, with progressive loss of quality.

The policies and practices of the National Science Foundation, of course, are designed to stave off in every possible way the worst implications of this dilemma. We try to ensure that large facilities and major instrumental capabilities will be widely accessible to the largest possible number of qualified scientists. This requirement is built in at the outset when we are planning major facilities, and we exercise oversight over their operations to ensure that the principle is honored. The same is true of some major laboratories maintained by other federal agencies.

It is appropriate here to mention one thing about policy formation which, although it's obvious enough, seems to be generally unappreciated. The federal policy-maker or planner must constantly tread a very fine line between being too timid and being reckless. He is usually laying plans for things to be done several years ahead, and he cannot know the political climate that will prevail at that time. If he plans too big, there may be great difficulty in completing the projects, and some may even have to be aborted. He will have raised expectations and gotten people to commit themselves to projects that end in frustration. On the other hand, if he is too timid and plans too small, various important projects, especially those that require long lead times, may be unnecessarily delayed or may never be carried out at all. The responsible policy-maker can make allowance for annual fluctuations and other short-term contingencies, but he really has no way of foreseeing major shifts of public preoccupation. In this respect, too, the private foundations, being somewhat insulated from public preoccupations, are able to "plan" with more confidence of continuity.

No matter how carefully we approach our task, not everyone will be satisfied. The system and its outcome are constantly exposed to the criticism of being "unbalanced" in one respect or another. Part of the difficulty arises from the fact that allocation takes place in many dimensions at once, including (in addition to those already discussed) such considerations as: the relative number of young, as against "established," scientists receiving support; support of "speculative" projects as against support of more conventional ones; distribution over classes of expenditure (salaries, equipment, supplies, communications, etc.); and the extent to which finer details of the allocation process are delegated to leadership at research-performing institutions.

With a few exceptions, the allocation process is not designed to yield consciously specified distributions with respect to the attributes on this list. Rather, these distributions fall out as by-products of the allocative judgments previously described. We allocate first in one dimension and then, sequentially, in several others. It is neither practical nor wise to attempt *a priori* specification of "balance" in every dimension. What can be done is to review the outcome from time to time from different points of view in order to verify that the overall process has not inadvertently produced unacceptable results. This we do.

Our efforts, of course, are continually under discussion by the National Science Board, the Congress, the Office of Management and Budget, several high-level advisory committees to the Foundation, and in the scientific press. The end result of all such endeavors is a web of interlocking compromises characterized by much uncertainty. None of those involved believes that the system works perfectly or even that he knows any criterion by which an optimum could be recognized.

The science allocation process is an inescapable task, and one that must be approached with great humility. We must bring to it a proper, but not unbalanced, emphasis upon those problems of society that are most acutely perceived at the moment.

Discussion

Dr. Sherman: I'd like to supplement Dr. Creutz's remarks with two observations that he might find difficult to make. The first has to do with what might happen in our utility-oriented culture, and particularly with the growing influence of the federal government on scientific activities and the policies governing them. It is the nature of what is happening in the legislative process recently with respect to authorization that limits two of the major federal agencies. If one includes the restriction of the Mansfield amendment on the Defense Department, that comes to three limitations. I'm thinking first of the one-year authorization that Dr. Creutz mentioned for the National Science Foundation, and the increasing restrictions made on legislation for cancer and heart research at the National Institutes of Health. What we see in the first instance are some very well-intentioned thoughts on the part of the National Science Foundation, National Science Board, and sympathetic members of the Congress to try to do something about what happened in the period from 1968 to 1970, when the financial fortune of science was declining.

Legislation was introduced by Mr. Daddario that changed the authorization in the period to a one year duration and in the level of possible funding. I feel that both in its anticipation and also in its experience that change was a major strategic error on the part of those who were very well-meaning in their attempt to do something about the problems of science at that time. A cycle of authority longer than one year is necessary.

There are two other issues to which the scientific community has paid entirely too little attention and which the Congress in its haste has also failed to heed. In both the cancer and the heart legislation for the NIH, the authorities with infinite duration that formed the provisions that set up the various institutes at the NIH, were shortened to three-year periods.

I suggest that for much scientific activity, particularly that involving rather basic efforts, as is true of both those agencies, three years is too brief, despite the need for periodic congressional overview. It demoralizes the members of the staff and stultifies their efforts when they have to go up before the Congress, as Dr. Creutz mentioned, four times a year, to two authorization legislative committees and to two appropriation committees for activities that probably are going to be many years in duration.

The other issue has to do with the morale of the staff, and the problems of recruitment and retention of first-rate individuals in positions of responsibility. All too frequently the scientific community has regarded individuals of this type in the capacity of mere handmaidens.

With the growing dependence on the federal government and the changing influences within that general area, unless the nation is able to recruit and retain the Ed Creutz's of the world for staffing federal agencies, this whole effort is going to be increasingly questionable in terms of achievement.

MARVIN ALBINAK (*Essex Community College, Baltimore, Md.*): Do you have any idea of how much of the total available funding of the NFS does go to speculative, new person—new place—new idea types of research? Does any significant amount of money go in that direction?

DR. CREUTZ: About 35 percent of our grants go to people who have not previously had a grant.

MR. ALBINAK: But that doesn't say anything about the allocation.

DR. CREUTZ: It would be difficult to define what is really a speculative proposal. In one of our divisions, the engineering division, we have research initiation grants, which can only be given to new people, that is, those who have had a PhD for less than five years.

MR. ALBINAK: Then these grants are similar to the starter grants given by the American Chemical Society.

DR. CREUTZ: Yes.

MR. ALBINAK: Are there any prescriptions or proscriptions in terms of types of institutions or types of activities?

DR. CREUTZ: No; according to law, of course we are to give "due regard to geographic distribution." Our first criteria are based on scientific merit. If we have two proposals of substantially equal merit we tend to make the grant to institutions in which there are fewer grants available.

DR. LANGER: Dr. Creutz, do the "virgin" applicants have to be supported by well-established academics?

DR. CREUTZ: No, not at all. It is just the purpose of the research initiation grant program, that the money be given to people who are not well known. Of course it's much more difficult to evaluate such people, and we have a special panel that meets once a year to look at this particular set of proposals. These beginning researchers usually do not have the support of any established investigators because they haven't published before. They just aren't known.

STEVEN ROSE: I feel a certain air of congratulatory complacency settling on us and I wish to disturb it at this point. Dr. Creutz, the way it seems from the center isn't necessarily the way it seems from the periphery. I have seen the panel review process from both ends.

I am concerned with the fact that you said earlier that you were not aware that there had been a serious questioning of the objectivity of research, and that there had been no "Lysenko scandals" raised in the context of American science. Yet many of the participants at this very conference have in fact charged science in this country with being elitist, sexist, and racist, which is evidenced by the technologies that come out of it. They have accused American science of producing devices and methodologies for the oppression of American people at home and the manipulation of foreign people abroad. I feel slightly surprised that the air of isolation at the center has in fact so completely insulated you from the very strong feeling that there are negative and antisocial outputs from science that is funded by the National Science Foundation and other agencies within the United States. Your optimistic view probably stems from your belief that all these agencies, and all these panelists, comprise a peer group of scientists moving projects forward that are somehow responsive to public needs and that this great scientific momentum is unrolling as a result of the consensual activities of all these 18,000 panelists. Instead, I would suggest that in terms of the real ways in which priorities are decided, the consensual process involves a much smaller number of people than 18,000 and this small number is interrelated or interlocked in a variety of ways. Because of these interlocks the number of decision-makers is smaller than it would seem. Furthermore, these decision-makers are slightly separated from the rest of "the scientific community." Thus the apparently diffuse activity of giving money has instead a rather monolithic quality, and end-products are produced which are of questionable value to the survival of mankind.

DR CREUTZ: In one sense science is elitist since only scientists can really judge the quality of science. Nonscientists can judge the *value* of science, but the quality of the proposed work can only be judged by scientists.

As far as the isolation that you speak of, Dr. Rose, it is quite true that the decisions are not made by people like you, who are kind enough to spend time in reviewing proposals. We do listen to your advice, but if we make a mistake, then we at the National Science Foundation must bear the responsibility of bad judgment; we can't shunt the responsibility onto the advisors. We do make the judgments on the basis of advice, but we include our own experience and our own advice.

DR. SIEKEVITZ: Has the National Science Foundation made any effort to review the research programs that were initiated 20 year ago, for example, to find out not only whether they fulfilled their initial mission-oriented purpose, but also whether there were any unanticipated consequences to society or science? Can we ever know what kind of an effect any given program will have except for a general one?

DR. CREUTZ: I think not, because the very nature of basic research is that you don't know where it's going. You have a general idea of where there are knowledge gaps, and you'd like to fill them in. We regard the support of basic research, and I think the Congress in general agrees with this, as a kind of insurance against the unknown problems of the future. The National Energy Program is one example of this kind of approach. Much of the money in energy research and development programs is going towards well defined projects, such as nuclear reactors, fusion programs, coal liquefaction and gasification, environmental effects, oil shale, solar energy, and geothermal energy, but a substantial and appreciable fraction of new money appropriated by the Congress this year for solutions to the energy problem went to basic research. When you start a basic research program, you may say it seems related to a problem of production of oil from oil shale because you're trying to understand better catalytic or chemical reaction processes, but you don't claim that if you solve this problem then you will automatically solve that problem. Basic research doesn't work that way. The basic researcher is not generally trying to solve a specific social problem; he's trying to add to the pool of knowledge upon which technology can be built. The basic researcher works to build a structure of great longevity.

It is true that basic concepts in science do change. In physics, for example, up until ten years ago there was every experimental reason to believe that the left/right handedness interreaction was not changed by any kind of nuclear reaction. Subsequently reactions were found where that is no longer true. So, although we look for fixed rules and fixed facts in science, we are also quite willing, if the evidence points that way, to accept that those laws are fixed only over a certain range of the variable.

To answer your question on evaluation of long-term consequences: Some studies have been carried out, but there is no question that there haven't been enough. A few years ago we supported a so-called traces study to look back at such technological results as the magnetic tape and the contraceptive pill to see what basic research they had depended on. It was interesting but not surprising to find that they could easily be traced to research at least 50 years old. Thus the long time scale and the longevity of the information add to the difficulty in evaluating the results of research. It would be very important, of course, in selection of research proposals if we could somehow weigh the probability that they would have a real positive effect on society. The best we can do now is to look at the past record of the investigator. We're often asked by Congress, for example, about the kind of detailed reports we get on the research. We don't insist on anything more than that the work be published in a scientific journal. We don't ask for a specific detailed report to the National Science Foundation; we wouldn't have time to read it. But in looking at the investigator's next proposal, a big factor that the reviewers and our own staff considers is the work he has done in the past and how it has affected the structure of science.

DR. ROTH: A limited, but systematic, type of evaluation was done by Arthur D. Little some fifteen years ago on the results of basic research sponsored by the Office of Naval Research. It traced a tree of knowledge and listed the investigators and work that branched from it, such as the research of people like Rabi. This was an interesting and valuable exercise.

BILL BENNETT (*Los Alamos, N.M.*): Dr. Creutz, I don't know whether we're looking for public policy to guide science or scientists to guide public policy. While the allocation of federal funds to research has to be an elitist process, I worry about the centralization implicit in that, the cost effectiveness, and allocation formulas that sound like equal opportunity employment legislation. I was encouraged at the comparison of the role of private foundations in the past to seek out neglected areas to put seed capital into. Whenever we attempt to impose some centralized elitist judgment on the allocation of funds, it seems to me that we're necessarily talking about applied research.

I don't think there has been a distinction made so far as to when we were talking about applied research as opposed to basic research. The remark was just made that the ground work of much recent progress was being laid perhaps 50 years ago, and I agree with Dr. Sherman that in that "time-frame" year-to-year funding and four hearings a year make life pretty miserable for the guy who is trying to stay at the workbench.

Elitest judgement should be spread out as much as possible. An organization does indeed have to earn its keep with an output of applied research programs. Perhaps every applied research task could have a tax associated with it, a fee that is left to the laboratory or project director to be dispersed among local researchers to support a basic research program.

I would suggest that the greatest advance in the delivery of health care services in the last 50 years is really the telephone, which can get the doctor there when he's needed.

DR. CREUTZ: It's true that this business of having four separate hearings a year means a lot of work for a busy staff. On the other hand, it does give us four times a year when we can be heard by Congress. Congress does listen the Committee, and the Committee staffs do see faces and hear ideas from the National Science Foundation four time a year. There is some value to that kind of exposure.

As to question of elitism: Not everybody is a great scientist; not everybody wants to be a scientist. There is only a small group of people who "do" good science, and who can do good science, so science will always be somewhat elite.

On the question of financial support to applied versus basic research I would offer the following remark. In any mission agency there is a man responsible for that mission and he must give all his attention to getting that mission done on time and within budget. He has to spend all his time and effort towards getting that project done in the best possible way. And that requires a different kind of personality from that of the man who thinks in terms of possible better ways and long-term consequences.

Part of the mistake of the mission-oriented agencies has been just that: they have put the responsibility of both the basic and the applied research under one manager. I believe that basic research would fare better if there was another person responsible for basic research in these mission-oriented agencies, rather than having one man have to worry about both.

MR. DECKER: I want to respond to Dr. Siekevitz's earlier question about grants to examine the social implications of past research. The Office of Exploratory Research Problem Assessment has just commissioned a retrospective technology assessment, which would go back to the time that a particular innovation like the automobile was first being developed and see whether its social impact could have been predicted. We would like to know if some of the sum of the social implications of such things as the telephone or hybrid corn can be traced out. It will be very interesting to learn the results of these grants.

DR. SIEKEVITZ: I think my question was somewhat misunderstood. In the last three years the National Science Foundation has been importuned by Congress to look into certain areas, such as solar energy, and it has received some funding for this—not much, because Congress has responded to other pressures, such as those exerted by the oil industry, to not support solar energy research.

What I would like to know is whether we can evaluate the decisions of the people who have to decide where to put the money on the basis of whether the research has been efficient in getting a result that can be applied. Can we make any predictions right now within a certain field of research? Is there any evaluation of this kind?

DR. CREUTZ: This is only a matter of judgement. The country has no policy as to how much of its energy should come from nuclear, thermonuclear, coal, or oil sources, so a good deal of my remarks were on just that point. There is no overall science policy in this country.

A lot of study must be retrospective. Fortunately priorities do change: not so long ago a lot of that money was going into the exploration of space; now, relatively little is. There is no way, particularly in basic research, to determine how much work should be done in physics, or in psychology, or in linguistics for optimal societal benefit. The sorting of priorities is a continually changing process.

We wish we had better ways to forecast the results of research. I would like to challenge one of your remarks: You claim that not much money is going into solar energy research. However, about 50 million dollars is going into it this year, and five years ago about one or more million dollars was apportioned. I believe that 50 million is quite a healthy amount of money for this type of research. I believe that you can only expand research in any area at a certain rate; I don't believe you can solve a problem by putting ten times more money into it.

STEVEN ROSE: I do find Dr. Creutz refreshingly frank, which is encouraging; but I want to come back to this question of elitism because he has said that science is elitest and it's highly desirable that it should be so, because not everyone can be a good scientist nor can everyone determine a good scientific project. Of course the general public can evaluate the results!

I want to challenge all of Dr. Creutz's assumptions. First, I think that a very large number of people who are not by contemporary definition, great scientists can be great scientists. Certainly I think that if we live in a society in which the general public is not put into a position to evaluate the content of a scientific project as well as its outcome, then we are in a very dangerous situation. Knowledge is power, as we all know. When knowledge is confined to a small proportion of people, power is confined to a small proportion of people. This has to be challenged.

If, in fact, what Dr. Creutz is saying about science is right, that it is inevitably elitist and therefore restricted to a small percentage of the population, then I believe that those people who challenge the values of science, and who say science is inevitably oppressive and should be stopped, are right and I would support them. However, I don't believe they are right because, Dr. Creutz, I don't think that you are right. I think we can have a science that is nonelitist, that is in the service of the broader mass of the people, and that is available to be done by a much broader mass of the people than your framework seems to suggest.

DR. LANGER: Dr. Creutz's paper has obviously raised some basic questions about applied science. He raised the problem of reading reports: I want to point out that the question of who reads reports is even more disturbing to a researcher than it may be to an agency. The question of retrospective review is a basic problem in all the sciences in this era. I wonder if it would be possible for the National Science Foundation and the federal agencies to take a sabbatical from research review. This might be healthy for the research field, and it certainly would be one possible way of trying to evaluate what has been accomplished in a three-, five-, or seven-year sabbatical period, not only to determine what has been done, but also to provide direction for new research.

DR. SHERMAN: I agree with Dr. Rose's concern about the dangers of elitism in relation to power, but I question the practicality of éducating the general public of the glories, the limitations, the challenges, and the responsibilities to be sufficiently informed on some of these matters. Even those who work 24 hours a day at trying to be informed fall grievously short of that kind of understanding.

LESTER TALKINGTON: Whether you set out to educate the general public or not, they are making these assessments all along, as reflected, for example, in congressional appropriations. It isn't a question of science controlling public policy; but there is a responsibility to help the public understand enough so that public policy can be more effective for the realization of the goals of science itself as well as for that of the public.

ACADEMIC INSTITUTIONS' ROLE, RESPONSE, AND REQUIREMENTS UNDER AN EFFECTIVE NATIONAL SCIENCE POLICY; OR, WHO PAYS THE PIPER?

Sidney G. Roth

New York University
New York, New York 10003

The proposition implicit in the title of this paper is based on at least three working assumptions:

1. There is an entity known as a national science policy or policies that may be defined "as the direction and planning of R & D, including social science research, by the interaction of the Government and the private sector."[1]
2. The policy(ies) can be measured in some operational terms to be identified as "effective."
3. There is a set of responses representing these institutions and their requirements to influence and implement these policies.

To set the stage for the possible understanding of what the parameters of this game are now or should be for the next decade or more, it is desirable to look briefly at the road this nation has travelled in almost 200 years of interaction between the federal government and higher education. Subsumed under "higher education" is that set of institutions that perform scientific research, teaching, and other services through themselves or allied units such as hospitals, research experimental stations, federally-financed research centers, and the like.

The Founding Fathers were well aware of the need for a strong scientific base for the fledgling nation. The Constitution, through Article I, Section 8, provides that Congress shall have the power "to promote the progress of science and useful arts by securing for limited times to authors and inventors the exclusive rights to their writings and discoveries." Thus, intellectual output and product represented an area in which the national government had a major interest. More directly, Franklin, Washington, Jefferson, Madison, and also John Quincy Adams attempted to create a national scientific university. However, Congress could not be moved.

Jefferson, the strong believer in an educated polis and influenced by science and mathematics, established his own institution in 1819 at Charlottesville near his well-beloved Monticello in Virginia. A few years later Congress engaged in a seemingly unending debate over whether to accept funds bequested by a relatively unknown British admirer of democratic ideals and revolution. James Smithson saw America as the fruitful soil for "an Establishment for the increase and diffusion of knowledge among men." A modest sum left in 1829 accrued to $500,000 by 1846 when at last the Smithsonian Institution was incorporated.

A unique American contribution to higher education emerged with the passage of the first Morrill Act in 1862 that established the so-called "land grant" college for the advancement of agricultural and the mechanical arts. From this network of institutions and their agricultural research stations have come many of the advances in agriculture that created a nation with an ample food supply—planted, tended, brought into being, but alas, not properly distributed—by a minor proportion of the population instead of the 75% or more previously required.

President Lincoln sought advice from scientific savants through the establishment of the National Academy of Sciences as a nongovernmental organization. This action was a war emergency measure but, moreover, as Alexander Dallas Bache, its first President, wrote in 1864, "The want of an institution by which the scientific strength of the country may be brought, from time to time, to the aid of the Government in guiding action by the knowledge of scientific principles and experiments, has long been felt by the patriotic scientific men of the United States."[2] In 1867, Joseph Henry, the Academy's brilliant leader, stated: "It is the first recognition by our Government of the importance of abstract science as an essential element of mental and material progress."[2]

In 1916, President Wilson took a similar step to make sure that the best scientific brains were corralled for national defense. Thus the National Research Council of the National Academy was established "to mobilize pure and applied science in support of the Government on an emergency basis."[3] However, World War II provided the vehicle for developing a radically different schema for mobilizing science for governmental purpose.

It was the beginning of a period that witnessed the flowering of science and science administration and policy: Senator Harley Kilgore's desire to have science applied on behalf of the national welfare, Dr. Vannevar Bush's efforts that eventually led to the National Science Foundation, President Eisenhower's moves in establishing within the White House the President's Science Advisory Committee and its companion Office of Science and Technology (the denouement being the disestablishment of this machinery by former President Nixon). Now, in 1974, the voice of science and technology is no longer in the Executive Office Building, but rather a block up G Street in the form of a second hat for Dr. Guy Stever, Director of the National Science Foundation, who also acts as the principal science advisor to the President. Perhaps our immediate past President was simply heeding the advice of C. P. Snow, who in his 1960 Godkin Lectures at Harvard intoned "Be on guard against the machinations of scientific advisors in high places,"[4]* rather than that of the National Academy of Sciences.†

Academic institutions have come a long way from the post-World War II days of the early 1950s, when Dr. Merle A. Tuve of the Carnegie Institution worried about the dependence of science based on government support or, for that matter, foundation beneficences and about its vulnerability to political pressures. He feared that this support might cause a betrayal of science. However, as Dr. Don K. Price has pointed out, while university administrators were worried about these and related issues, they in fact had no alternative.[5] He indicated that perhaps universities were in a position exemplified by the young lady from Kent who "knew what it meant—but she went." Despite these numerous warnings of loss of independence, the interface of government-university science in obligations has grown from $138 million in 1953 to $2,763 million by 1974, a 20-fold increase in 21 years.

This backward glance seems to illuminate an important principle reinforced

---

* This moral developed from Sir Charles' evaluation of Lord Cherwell's "culpable" behavior in the early days of World War II on the issue of whether Britain should invest in developing radar.

† The National Academy of Sciences Ad Hoc Committee on Science and Technology Report, *Science and Technology in Presidential Policymaking—A Proposal*, states "We recommend that a Council of Science and Technology be established as a staff agency in the Executive Office of the President (page 6).

through periods of emergency and calm: the federal government has continued to rely upon academic institutions for the advancement of science and technology for the national good. This principle gets implemented in diverse ways and with varying degrees of consultation between governmental decision-makers and representatives of higher education. It is clear that if the nation's existence is threatened by war, the ranks close quickly and common goals are attacked with vigor. However, when the country has a lower order of crisis, then the differences between government and academia assert themselves; each sector seeks to emphasize its distinctive inputs to science policies while seeking to influence the contribution of resource from the other sector. Nevertheless, the primary thrust for this dynamic movement generally originates in the Executive Branch of the government with countervailing forces in the Congress. Academia has the opportunity to make itself heard, but principally as a reacting body to both of these governmental vectors. Colleges and universities seem to be in continual frustration over basic science policy issues, generally because they can only react to decisions made by the Office of Management and Budget (OMB) or by Congress. They are not the whole of society but only a part. And, their goals are not identical with those of government.

National science policies are important for several reasons: not only for the goals they represent but also for the scale of resource to be allotted for implementation and the determination of which sector undertakes to carry out these policies. We are concerned here with an allocation of a major resource to science and technology by the Federal budget: almost $18 billion in the 1974 fiscal year and an indicated $19.6 billion for the current fiscal year. As has already been noted, higher education's share of this obligation is significant indeed.

To illustrate the issue, Dr. Edward E. David, the last Director of the Office of Science and Technology, explicated the science goals for the 1973 fiscal year in essentially the following terms: (1) Overall national research and development efforts must be adequate to keep us competitive intellectually, economically, and functionally. (2) Federal R & D programs must be focused on top priority needs. (3) The nation must receive full value from its large expenditures on R & D. (4) Our extensive capabilities in science and technology must be effectively utilized.

These goals are not very operational, but they eventually get translated into such terms with full impact upon academic institutions.

The Executive branch, principally through the Office of Management and Budget, establishes a ceiling on expenditures which it expects each of its departments and agencies to meet for planning purposes. This total limitation is based generally on assumptions underlying the economy, total or nontotal employment, expected level of government revenues, etc. This process leads to a budgetary document that the President presents to Congress by the end of January of each year asking for a given sum. Thus, in the 1975 fiscal year President Ford wants to limit spending to $300 billion. Congress, through its many committees charged with oversight of the authorization and appropriation of funds in each field, holds hearings to determine the adequacy of the presidential request in terms of its perception of national needs. To these hearings are invited federal officials responsible for the programs being covered by the budgetary requests, as well as expert witnesses from academic and other sectors who try to influence the decisions. This process is time-consuming and of such fragmentation that rarely do responsible officials have an overall view of what they have voted upon. This year Congress is planning to reorganize its committee structure. Its objective is to develop a unified look at the budget rather than only a fragmented version that has made it difficult to keep appropriations in line with policy objectives.

Thus, academia has the opportunity to influence these policy implementation decisions in a variety of ways. The many Washington-based associations, principally at One Dupont Circle, representing higher education and science, request a distinguished faculty member, president, or other official to present evidence on their behalf at a congressional hearing. There is considerable interplay between groups such as the American Council on Education, the National Association of State Universities and Land Grant Colleges, the Association of American Universities, plus many others, and Congressional committees. Also, an enlightened committee chairman will seek edification for himself and his colleagues by inviting leading scientists and educators to testify or present background papers on a scientific field. Congressional hearings are replete with scholarly presentations of this nature.

Another opportunity for academic scientists and administrators to influence policy is through science or advisory boards such as the NIH Advisory Committees or Councils, the National Science Board, and as program officers in one of the operating agencies. However, one must remember that neither academia nor science is of one mind on almost any policy issue other than "Give us more!"

An important policy of long standing in the federal government is the development of the basic research capability of the nation through the colleges and universities rather than through separate or governmental research institutes, such as those found in Germany and other countries. Of the approximately $17.5 billion expended by federal agencies for R & D in the 1974 fiscal year, almost $7 billion was for research, basic and applied, with the former estimated at $2.421 billion. Of this last number, colleges and universities were the recipient of 38% with another 11% going to the federally funded R & D centers (FFRDCs) administered by universities. Thus the academic community had responsibility for some $1.203 billion for basic research alone.

This process of granting large sums for academic science basic research has posed a policy issue squarely at the federal-higher education intersection. Basic research is generally proposed to an agency by a faculty member whose scientific interests match those of the hoped-for sponsor. While the latter's program may be spelled out in broad terms through budget documents and position papers, the actual implementation occurs via the award process. Does the agency fund a given proposal or not?

In major institutions such as the National Institutes of Health and the National Institute of Mental Health, the awards or grants are committed through "peer reviews," principally undertaken by leading academic scientists who are the panel members. They are primarily concerned with the quality of the scientific protocol being proposed, the qualifications of the research team requesting support, etc. In general, their assumption is that good science is good for the nation and therefore good for the NIH. Critics of this process believe that the goals and policies of the particular agency employing this method for awarding grants may be, and are, sometimes skewed. In other words, their concern is that the program direction is removed from the persons charged with such responsibility to the sphere of academies and other consultants. Thus, the peer-review system came under attack some two years ago and contract procedures were instituted for research, especially in cancer.

While the peer-review system seems to be intact currently, the basic issue remains. Its resolution is important for all parties concerned.

Another dimension has entered university science life through the urging and flow of federal manna in the applied research sphere. This sector in the 1974 fiscal year accounted for another $952 million, representing 22% of all such expenditures by federal agencies, with 18% going through campuses and allied units and only 4% through FFRDCs.

Now what are these inputs and influences upon academia? They're troublesome, worrisome, pervasive, distorting, and possibly dangerous to the intellectual well-being of these institutions. Yet there isn't a major academic center that hasn't gained from this interaction or could thrive without them in these days. For example, of the 140-odd medical schools now extant, there probably is not one that wouldn't suffer a major "surgical trauma" if federal funds were withdrawn or cut by 20% or more. In the past two or three years, with major cutbacks and withdrawals of funds threatened by the White House, the health professions and medical centers convinced the congressional decision-makers, but probably not the OMB seers, that a major collapse was imminent if in fact the funds for research, training and manpower development, capitation, and facilities were curtailed. The AAMC rallied the forces of reason or perhaps of persuasion around their champions on the Hill—Senator Edward Kennedy and Representaive Paul Rogers—and beat back the cutting edge of the OMB and their devastating impoundments. Of course, this past year was unusual for other reasons! But even before that Senator Javits and others were convinced that several medical centers were threatened with monetary anemia and an emergency fund of $100 million was made available to save these schools.

On the broader academic science and technology scene, the higher education community has responded consistently to national programs for meeting social needs. Most recently these goals were expressed in terms of health, energy, environment, urban problems, transportation, and education. Yet, after an input of increasing federal resources for research and training in these primary areas, the flow slowed, beginning in 1969, and smaller sums were made available in 1972 or 1973, especially if one measured the input in constant dollars. Academic institutions were left holding an expanded, expensive bag that they couldn't possibly afford. Who was to pay the piper? Under the "new federalism" of revenue-sharing the states were to pick up a larger share, but higher education in general seems not to have shared in this sharing.

This on-again, off-again tactic is one that imperils the fiscal well-being of institutions that play in the arena. The National Science Foundation and Office of Education as well as the National Institutes of Health have jolted academia with unilateral decisions of this nature. This phenomenon has two facets: (1) programs are diminished or wiped out on a very short time-scale and (2) major shifts in emphases are instituted. Thus, the curtailment of training programs sponsored by the several federal health agencies truly did not take into account the lead times which govern academic institutions. The significant financial input to cancer, heart, and lung research at the apparent expense of ongoing programs in other health fields, where major laboratories and scientific teams had been developed, raised the spectre of mass displacement of personnel within medical schools and centers without the resource to accomplish this move. These instances illustrate the need to realign the short-term actions of the federal government with the essentially longer cycle required by academia. 'Tis a strange partnership that has developed.

A second impact is the influence of the need for solutions to real-life problems that the agencies regard as important. For the past several years, RFPs, solicitations for proposals, and other delicacies have been coming down the scientific pike. The most prestigious agencies, including NIH and NSF, are asking universities to examine, analyze, and propound solutions to issues and problems posed by the solicitor. This is a new experience for most academic scientists and their institutions, which are discipline- rather than problem- or issue-oriented. There are several reasons for this move of applied research on the campuses: (1) basic research results should be applied now to pressing societal problems; (2) such issues as energy, population, pollution, and transportation are draining the nation's resources; (3) technology transfer from campus to industry to society can be expedited if academia will cooperate in developing appropriate forms of research organization.

This last proposition may be one whose time has come. Some 12 years ago, James Webb, then-Administrator of NASA, tried his best to get academic institutions to develop interdisciplinary groups, to work with industry to have the latter utilize the science and technology developed on campus. In general, he was responsible for the concept of technological utilization or "fall-out." NASA made a number of major grants for such purpose, but campus resistance was too great for this academic-industrial link to flourish. At approximately the same time, Dr. Herbert Hollomon, then in the Department of Commerce, pulled out his State Technical Assistance Act, whereby schools would work with industry. After a few years Congress became unhappy with this facade of cooperation, and Dr. Hollomon departed. Both NIH and NSF have developed their own forms of applied programs. After all, health research consists of basic science as well as the application of such principles. Thus, NIH justifies its role with many elements of higher education other than the professional health schools. And these formerly mentioned faculties welcome the opportunity to be of assistance. NSF has sought, via the needed change in legislation, to entice academia into applied research on a grand scale. After a year or so of finding their way through the Interdisciplinary Research Relevant to Problems Society (IRRPOS), program, colleges and universities found a new entity, Research Applied to National Needs (RANN), that had been given more than 10% of NSF's budget of some $700 million. Major problem areas are listed to which institutions may respond through forming cross-disciplinary teams to help develop solutions that are found workable to the eventual consumer, industry, or governmental agency, that must be represented in the study. From one point of view, this is a healthy development because universities will have to seek ways to solve their organizational difficulties in trying to put together such teams. If these efforts do in fact contribute to the development of basic knowledge, and are more speedily applied than would be the case without this push, they are positive. If, however, they detract from the primary purposes of higher education and tend to put universities into the arena of solving short-term problems, there is a mismatch.

An area where academic institutions can play a unique role is popularly called "public understanding of science." This rubric assumes greater importance each year for many reasons: the large investment in science and technology, the considerable preoccupation by Congress and other agencies at all levels of government with scientifically-based phenomena, the impact of science and technology upon each individual in this industrial society, and the need for a truly general educational program to comprehend the positive and negative contributions that science does and can make through peacetime and wartime technology.

One concern shared by many within the academic community is the misunderstanding of science and its promise by the general public and by some otherwise intelligent legislators. This phenomenon has led to a distrust of science and scientists that has been reflected in appropriations for specific programs and may well affect the place of science and universities within the society. The need for a program of widespread education should be one of the primary elements of public policy at this time.

Despite a variety of attempts by many organizations, large and small, no truly mass movement has developed that bears the message of science and its role in society. Diverse efforts through the National Science Foundation, the American Association for the Advancement of Science, the Federation of Atomic Scientists, the New York Academy of Sciences, and others have reached various population sectors but have not stimulated the necessary thinking required to make this a successful program. Here is a large arena in which academic institutions of all kinds and levels can utilize their skills to develop imaginative and informative programs on issues ranging from a basic understanding of science through atomic energy, pollution, population, and every other critical issue facing the society. The talent would seem to be available; the technologies are present; what seems to be required is a marriage of the proper resources to accomplish this task for the millions of people "who need to know."

Finally, the use of universities for the solution of problems is only one side of the science policy coin. These institutions represent the nation's basic intellectual resource. As such, they are more than contractors for the federal establishment. For years, university administrators have tried to educate Congress and the Executive Branch to recognize the need for stable funding. Only in the past ten years has the government legally pursued its role to advance higher education and the intellectual development of these institutions as organic entities. In the past, this was bootlegged through research grants. But the importance of these institutions to the society can only be ensured through programs that provide support for their general well-being on a long-term basis. That formula or set of formulas has not yet been discovered.‡ The national priorities seem to place this issue well down the list; academia has not found the arena of total agreement on those issues that divide it. Further, the spokesmen for higher education have not been as effective or as numerous in their approaches to the nation's decision-makers as have representatives of other sectors. In short, the interface of science and politics, higher education and politics, has become a tangle of ad hoc solutions without too many generally accepted principles. This is probably one of the more compelling problems that must be solved shortly so that the country may be provided with a sound basis for intellectual, ethical, and material progress. In Harvey Brooks' words, "It should be national policy to help create a university environment to which some of the best minds of each generation will be attracted."[6] Anything short of this is failure!

In summary, it would appear that the development of national science policies is not the sole province of federal officials. Yet the channels for communication and participation are not as well-defined as they should be. Too much of the process is performed on an ad hoc basis and shifts in goals occur without appropriate debate. Academic and allied institutions are major participants in implementing policies; their principal role has been as *reactor* to governmental requests rather than as *initiator* of policy and programs. Further, perceptions of goals, the length of time necessary to achieve these goals, and the methods by which these programs are moved to achieve these goals are viewed differently, in noncrisis periods especially,

‡ The Carnegie Commission on Higher Education, through several of its reports, addressed this crucial problem to delineate alternative courses of action. Anyone wishing to pursue this issue would be assisted by reading: *Institutional Aid: Federal Support to Colleges and Universities; Quality and Equality;* and *Priorities for Action: Final Report of the Carnegie Commission on Higher Education.*

by government officials and academic representatives. The mismatch becomes intensified when new procedures are initiated for scientific research or when ongoing programs are curtailed. At the focus of these differences is the use or misuse of universities for governmentally-supported programs on a large scale without fundamental recognition by the Executive Branch and Congress of the integral nature of the academic institution and structure and of the need to nurture this resource and not only those elements immediately involved in a particular research program. Despite these negative features, the nation has somehow produced a working system of unreliable components that functions, involves huge resources in manpower and facilities, and produces an output of unmatched scientific developments.

REFERENCES

1. An Inventory of Congressional Concern with Research and Development (page IV), 89th Congress, 2nd Session, Part 2. October 11, 1967. U.S. Government Printing Office. Washington, D.C.
2. SEITZ, F. Statement before House Committee on Science and Astronautics (page 16), Hearings Before the Subcommittee on Science, Research, and Development, 88th Congress, 1st Session. 1964. U.S. Government Printing Office. Washington, D.C.
3. *Ibid.*: 17.
4. SNOW, C. P. 1961. Science and Government. Harvard University Press. Cambridge, Mass.
5. PRICE, D. K. 1954. Government and Science.: 87. New York University Press. New York, N.Y.
6. Science Policy and the University. 1968. Harold Orlans, Ed.: 66. Brookings Institution.

A CRITIQUE OF SOCIAL SCIENCE MODELS OF CONTEMPORARY SOCIETY: A FEMININE PERSPECTIVE

June Nash

*Department of Anthropology
The City College of New York
New York, New York 10031*

The social sciences disseminate understanding through models or constructs of the segments of social life they study. These constructs may serve as analytic charts or as ideology. As new segments of the population enter into the discourse, there is a tendency to open discussion on the models that have served as tools of the trade. Such a critique began when colonized people entered the professional social sciences formerly dominated by the colonizer. Now, with the advance in research done by women another critical approach is beginning. This paper tries to assess the importance of the models in shaping public policy in development programs and the way in which the feminine critique of the stereotypes reveals the ideological content of the models.

Recent investigations have revealed the extent of the distortion in our understanding that results from omission of the female population, or to accepting stereotypes as fact. Political scientists and historians note the absence of commentary on women's political activities, taking note only when they fall into accepted stereotypes as camp-followers or housewives clamoring for more consumption goods.[1-5] Literary critics, analysts of popular culture, and experts on the family show how female protagonists are distorted to fit stereotypes held by the male.[6,7] Anthropologists have begun to focus on female culture heretofore treated as the infrastructure servicing and maintaining male culture,[8-11] although earlier studies were published that have set the pace.[12,13] Economists and sociologists are beginning to take into account women's economic activity, much of which has not been calculated in the gross national product since it never directly entered into the market, and their work reveals the consequent distortion in economic indices.[14-20]

These studies in progress and recently published suggest that the major conceptual formulations applied in the analysis of developing countries are similarly skewed by having ignored one-half of the population. Some Marxist analysts have forgotten Marx and Engels' dictum that the status of women is the measure of progress and have treated exploitation only within the production setting in industry. The fact that the women who service the work force and render them available to industry do not receive a wage signified that they were outside the arena of exploitation by capital and consequently did not have a socially recognized role in protest movements, as Dalla Costa and James[21] point out. Dependency analyses neglect the paradigm of behavior appropriate to the relations of subordination between "developed" and "developing" nations in a world market as reinforced in the nuclear family where patron-client, male-female, and child-parent relations provide the models for subservience and acceptance of an inferior lot in life.[22] Development models are primarily concerned with women insofar as their reproductive and consumption functions affect savings in the phase of capital accumulation. They have failed to devise a measure of the nonmarket contributions made by women, and as a consequence they have consistently undervalued their contribution to the productive process. Most theories of modernization assume that man's status is the universal measure of change and ignores the uneven progress for women in developing countries.[23-25]

In short, social scientists have until recently accepted stereotypes that have blinded them to the changing reality of women's participation in the economic, political, and social life of society. This failure is especially dangerous when social scientists are called upon to formulate public policy. Crippled by archaic views inherited from colonial and early independence days, the development programs are designed with the male population taken as the activist sector and the females the passive bystanders. Even worse, male views of appropriate female roles are imposed in areas where women have shared the basic productive functions of the society with men and where development policies mean a step backward for women.

Social scientists have played the role of ideologists rather than analysts, sustaining the notion of progress implied in modernization and development and perpetuating social structures constrictive to women's participation in economic, social, and political life. Their "objective" analyses in fact reinforce stereotypes of women as wives, mothers and lovers, even when these roles are reenacted on a stage where all the props—the male as protector and breadwinner—are gone. Women socialized to perceive the world with male models have contributed to the errors and fantasies contained in the persisting mythology of sex roles and social structures. They proved their ability by conforming to the models of reality structured by established figures in the field and on the basis of criteria set by men. These include: (1) making objective statements of social reality, divorcing the personal perspective from the subject of discourse; (2) eliminating empathetic understanding from observation; and (3) accepting the terms of universal discourse without recognizing the particularistic elements that influence the field of observation. By accepting these rules, women became honorary brothers in the men's house of social science discourse.

As their numbers have increased and as the consciousness of mutual problems has underwritten their own sense of self, women social scientists have begun to question what anthropologists call the male models imposed on their discipline[26-28] or what sociologists call the failure of paradigms.[29] They have called for a reassessment of the research methods in the choice of samples and of the analyses, bringing into question the male bias in choice of problems, the pretenses of universality in studies that often take only one-half or less of the population into view, and the models predicated on androcentric perspectives. Current studies that bring women into focus are cultivating that binary view, neglected in the past, that most women share with members of oppressed groups, and that comes from what W.E.B. Dubois conceived of as "double consciousness," or seeing both sides because of the need to survive subject to the will of the dominant.[28] In order to correct our vision of reality, we must make sexual perspective an objective part of our analysis.

MODELS OF SOCIAL REALITY IN LATIN AMERICA

Modernization

Latin American studies in the 1950s and '60s, were dominated by Weberian and neocolonial models of modernization and development exported along with the consumer products of North American firms. Progress was measured by indices of energy consumption, of gross national product, crude birth and death rates, and some gross measures of cultural levels: illiteracy, educational attainment, percentage of radio sets, etc.[30] Figures failed to reveal the distribution of income, the purchasing power of wages, or the domestic consumption and intrafamilial distribution of wage returns. Even worse, there are large poverty-blighted areas and even entire countries that did not even have these crude statistics.

Development was the goal, a development predicated on industrialization and modeled on the western drive to profit from the production of more and more goods even at the expense of a byproduct of people made useless by automation. Modernization, linked to a philosophical assumption that progress is measurable in terms translated into a rising GNP and increasing consumption of energy resources, has negative aspects in the depletion and destruction of natural resources and the wasteful exploitation of human labor. Value is assessed only in relation to those goods and services that enter into a market and consequently it is measured by narrow economic constructs.

The emphasis on market factors as an index of progress leads to a devaluation of goods and services that do not enter into a market. In the process of modernization, women's products and services have been ignored and in some cases eliminated from the market as their handicrafts yield to the competition of factory-made goods. Their services have been confined to domestic spheres that no longer are centers of productivity as they were during the household stages of production.[15] Excluded from the modernizing sectors of the society because of persisting domestic responsibilities and exclusion from higher-paying jobs, their range of economic and political activities has been narrowed rather than expanded in the process of modernization. The widening of horizons assumed to be the correlate of modernizing societies when only men are taken into consideration, becomes its opposite with the increasing privatization of women's activities.[31] Unmeasured by indices of modernization, women's work is consequently devalued by those who concern themselves with progress. Where modernization and its effect on women have been taken into account, at least in the Middle East where the differences between male and female lives are so salient, the concern is more with the inhibiting effect a "traditional" wife will have on a "transitional" male entering modern life[32] and Western models of the consumer-oriented housewife are taken as the epitome of feminine independence and liberation.[33]

Comparative statements about modernization and the gains attributed to industrialization often take as their base line earlier stages in mature economies. Assertions of progress based on such comparisons ignore the fact that in the initial phases of industrialization there was a process of debasement of labor in comparison with preindustrial stages. Industrialization was not progress for the artisan left without employment and forced into proletarian dependency. Women, who were an important part of the preindustrial artisan work force, not only lost a market for their products, but also were excluded from some of the new opportunities, ill-paid as they were, in the industrial sector. Thus the conclusions of Rosen and La Raia[34] that women in industrial communities have a greater sense of personal efficacy, enjoy more egalitarian relations with their husbands, place a greater emphasis on independence and achievement in the socialization of children, and perceive the world in a more activist perspective, ignore an earlier period in history when women fulfilled a vital function in agriculture, in gathering of forest products or in fishing as well as in contemporary societies where household economies persist. As Wertheim[35] points out, "The subordinate position of women is, therefore, rather an urban phenomenon and widespread in oriental commercial districts. For rural societies, this subordination of women certainly cannot be taken as an omniprevalent characteristic."

The mystique of modernization begins with the Weberian assumption that the past must be replaced with the new, that the rational must supersede the irrational equated with the traditional order. Karl Deutsch[36] sums up this view of modernization as "the process in which major clusters of old social, economic and psychological commitments are eroded and broken and the people become available for new patterns of socialization and behavior." The key to modernization, he goes on to say, is exposure to aspects of modern life through demonstrations of machinery, buildings, consumer goods in response to mass media, changes of residence, urbanization, change from agricultural occupations, literacy and the growth of per capita income.

Eisenstadt[37] is an even stronger advocate of progress implied by industrialization along lines of western capitalism. In his view of modernization as a breakdown of traditional ascriptive criteria of status, he ignores the sex ascription that continues to operate in most modern societies. Praising the advance in highly differentiated political structures, he forgets that women have less chance to influence decision-making than was the case when more political activities stemmed from the household base. Extolling the spread of potential political power to wider groups, he fails to mention that these are associations of men which explicitly or implicitly exclude women in unions, political parties and even cooperatives and collectives designed to gain greater participation of the masses in productive processes.

When we bring the oppressed sectors of society into this picture, we threaten the social structuring of reality perceived from a dominant elite viewpoint. Those who recognize these systemic failures due to discrimination based on ascriptive factors and still retain the ideal traditional to modern dichotomy attribute them to "social lag."[71] This evades the issue of the fundamental contradictions in capitalism which require ever more restrictive channels for distributing the rewards of a system that concentrates power and control over production and the profits accruing from it.

Modernization cannot be equated with liberalization, with universalistic criteria, greater rationality, and recognition of achievement so long as over half of the population is reduced in their spheres of action, participation and rewards. We cannot assume progress and rationality in a system that must generate more propaganda and more appeals to biological determinism to maintain over half the population in subordination. The Parsonian pattern variables of modernization are revealed as an ideology validating modernization predicated along lines of private capitalist exploitation.

The differential impact of modernization on women and men has not been noted until recently because women have not been part of the interviewing sample nor have they been senior investigators in research. Gans and coworkers[38] point out that David Smith and Alex Inkeles, in his study of modernization (1966) interviewed 5,500 people in Argentina, Chile, India, Pakistan, Israel and Nigeria, none of whom were women, yet their OM scale purported to be a comparative sociopsychological measure of individual modernization. Joseph Kahl[25] perpetuated this error when he and his helper interviewed 1300 men in Brazil and Mexico and gave his book the universalistic title *The Measurement of Modernism: A Study of Values in Brazil and Mexico*. Weiner's anthology on modernization[39] includes only male contributors dealing primarily with the male segment of the population.

Robert Wood, the only author to mention the "nonparticipants" in modernization, included "hardcore minority of marginal men, displaced workers, and increasingly old people,"[40] but failed to mention women.

Unlike other segments of the population, women are consistently neglected in samples because of an assumed universalistic criterion based on men as central actors in the system. It is not an oversight to exclude them from the sample, but a fundamental premise of a social science in which men are the measurement of change. When we take women into account in studying modernization, as Gans and coworkers[38] did in their interviews of 322 wives along with 623 men, we are made aware of the fact that women do not exhibit the expected correlates of modernization. They lag behind men in socioeconomic status, education, mobility and occupational choice. Excluded from the managerial and productive work in the modernizing sectors, they are likely to resist changes that are interpreted as threatening. Failing to analyze the objective conditions which make for the conservative attitudes attributed to women, these characteristics are attributed to the feminine nature, a mystique of timidity and passivity. We must go further, questioning the model of modernity itself and its failure to reveal the selective discrimination of the process in which segments of the population are favored or rejected in advanced capitalist industrialization.

There is one arena in which women are permitted and even encouraged to participate in modernization: as consumers in an ever more elaborated scale of preferences and products. Consumer ideology of modernization gives an illusion of progress and movement within a superstructure of revolution defined technologically and yet antithetical to adaptive social change, as Mitchell[41] and Mattelart[42] show. Women are the target of consumer economics of modern business. By their constant consumption of changing styles and trends they maintain the rising demands required to sustain sales and profits. Women are, as Mattelart shows, the carriers of the gadgets and styles that make them seem the manipulators rather than the victims of modernity.[42] Even their liberation drives are absorbed in a consumer cult in which the right to smoke Virginia Slims or redecorate a living room in the latest mode mark the pinnacle of success.

Women's function in maintaining high consumption levels validates the productive structure based on exploitation and denial of a productive role for them in the modernizing sector. Male advertisers have finessed the threat of real liberation of women by imposing their ideas upon the movement: freer sex and greater consumption through ever more faddish clothing to make women themselves a more desireable object of consumption. It is no coincidence that a rising hemline was associated with rising demands by women for greater independence, nor that women's liberation movements in the United States and Latin America expressed their first protest against the use of women as sexual objects in the communication industry.[41]

Modernity, or entry into the expanding consumer market of man-made goods, is predicated on a development in which the goals are defined by the markets of the capitalist producing centers. Their films, magazines, and canned TV programs provide the models for stimulating consumer demand in the periphery, creating needs where there were undefined wants and unsatisfied aspirations, exacerbating the economic dependency through an ever-increasing debt structure mediated through the balance of trade deficits. Developmentalist solutions called for import substitution to check the flow of receipts from primary goods back to the consumer markets of the center, but the markets they served cater to the luxury-consuming upper classes and put added burdens on the trade imbalance by calling for sophisticated machinery made in the industrial center as well as imported raw materials unavailable in the new production centers.[43] Even the lower classes entered as consumers of products unavailable or produced at great social cost in their countries: cosmetics, dentrifices, patent medicines, crockery, cooking ware —items that replaced indigenous products available at little or no cost before the invasion of foreign goods. The rising demand for foreign goods—ranked higher because they were foreign—minimized the market for local goods. Since they were often produced in household-based crafts, fit in along with domestic and child-rearing tasks, the loss of these low-cost productive centers increased the dependency of local producers on the mass-production market. The multipurposed, highly adaptive household productive system is the victim of development concentrating on industrial settings in both rural and urban areas.

Women's work, which supplemented and sustained the family income and gave stability and a modicum of independence to the primary breadwinner, was devalued and in many cases eliminated. Nonetheless, the kind of indices used to prove the greater rationality of the industrial system supported the development sense of progress. Because more goods entered the market, as household-based crafts were eliminated, the GNP grew and confirmed the choices made. When reformist pressures led to land reform or other measures that tipped the scale toward self-sufficiency, the falling GNP proved the inefficiency of the change. When, for example, the Mexican government in the 1930s yielded to the demands of the peasantry to implement the revolutionary laws of 1927 on land reform, agricultural production fell, not because there was a lower crop return, as some concluded, but because subsistence agriculture satisfied the immediate needs of the producer and as a consequence was not tallied in the GNP.

Dependency

Dependency, cultivated in the world market as well as the internal market, is a byproduct of the shift from artisan and household production to industrialization controlled from metropolitan centers of production. The shift was particularly marked in its effect on women. Dependent on the uncertain earnings of a dependent wage earner, their subservience was even more marked than that of the industrial worker. Dependency theory rarely links this relationship to the chain of dependencies forged in the international capital market. Looked at internally, women's subordination to a male breadwinner appears to be a factor of personal oppression, not of capitalist exploitation. However women commentators have demanded that the extension of exploitation by private capitalists be recognized in the domestic sphere. Flora Tristan[44] summed up the exploitation of both working class and bourgeois women as the kept servants of men of all classes in the words, "The most oppressed man can oppress another human being, who is his wife. She is the proletarian of the very proletariat." When she broke free from French petit bourgeois family life in the early nineteenth century, she began to voice the suffering and needs of the working class. Her sympathy extended to the prostitutes, the beggars, the imprisoned women of London and France, who, in Marxist analysis were relegated to the lumpenproletariat and hence were of little import to the class struggle.

The dependent victims of industrial progress are still largely ignored by both radical and conservative male analysts. Dalla Costa and James[26] Largia and Demoulin,[45] James,[46] and Jelin[47] reveal how women's unpaid labor in production and reproduction extends the exploitation of industry into the privacy of the home. In the United States the unpaid work of women runs up to 99.6 hours a week (Chase National Bank, quoted by Mitchell [Reference 41:102]). More studies are needed of the costs to industry of dining halls and dormitories, the time lost because of unstructured leisure, in order to assess the relative costs of servicing and maintaining a work force in the nexus of the family in comparison with commercial services. The family is implicitly recognized as a cheaper solution, as revealed by industrial relations managers' attempts to foster the nuclear family by subsidizing reproductive costs and direct payment to workers for family dependents.[22] At the same time, we must recognize that until there is a valid, socially recognized basis for domestic services, the contribution women make will not be assessed even by constructing market indices of their input because of its elusive quality. More important than the domestic services they provide, women serve as instruments of social control, as the Schwendingers[48] point out, socializing the present and future members of the labor force to accept their roles in industry. They quote the early liberal ideologists of the family, Ward[49] and Thomas,[50] who perceived women as a factor in social production whose management of the working class men in their off-hours decreased social expenses and improved the efficiency and functioning of industry.

The dependency of women in the political and social life of the community and nation reinforces the dependency relations at higher socioeconomic levels. This stems from the material conditions impinging on women within the domestic unit and the social relations that result from them. On the one hand, there is the pressure on women to bear the major responsibility for life and death processes. Cut off from a social network where they can share these burdens, especially after their "liberation" from the extended kin group, women often turn to religious and political institutions to share these burdens. This factor, rather than an inherent conservatism, causes them to support the very institutions in which they are oppressed.

On the other hand, the workingman has less latitude to act politically given the domestic dependents he must support. His vulnerability, multiplied by that of his family, reduces his ability to react to exploitation even when he is fully conscious of his class interests. The low margin of subsistence and the high debts deriving from consumer dependency reduce his chances for planning ahead, a feature often ascribed to personality or cultural factors[51] rather than economic conditions. I have seen workers in the tin-mining communities of Bolivia who resist their wives' entry into employment, despite the family needs for additional income, for fear they would lose control over their wives or that their working companions would scorn them.

A penetrating analysis of the internal structuring of roles that support external dependencies and maintain status quo systems of expropriation is needed as a refinement of existing theory.

Marginality

The increasing concentration of capital and its impact on the working class structure indicates that the ever-growing sector not only of the unemployed but also of the unemployable is a persistent feature of modernizing societies. This sector, since it is not competitive for jobs in highly capitalized industry, does not serve as a reserve labor supply in the classic Marxist sense, but simply as a depressant on wages for redundant services.[52] Evidence from many of the technologically advanced sectors of the society as well as from governmental decision-making seems to justify this kind of analysis. However, if we accept the structural base of marginality as developed by José Nun,[52] we see how large segments of the population, both male and female, are permanently displaced from productive work by technology, as capital-intensive industry penetrates into economies that do not have the expansion potential for absorbing displaced manual labor in any but low-paid service capacities. To include women as a separate category in this segment minimizes the impact of the analysis.

Further, to classify women's role in production and reproduction as marginal means that one accepts the distortion implied in consumer advertising of their fundamental activities as providers of food, health and welfare as frivolous and the woman in her domestic role as a plaything.[41] So long as these functions were socially supported and figured as the main goal of production in a household economy, women's activities in the home continued to be centrally important to the total productive sphere.[53, 54] Since industry has taken over much of the basic production, women's sphere of activity has been devalued.

The jobs that women perform in the modern sectors of the economy to which they have gained entry—as secretaries, assistants in research, communications supervisors, education—have a kind of "reproductive" function, as Mitchell[41] shows. They mediate between men in the nerve centers of complex societies, and are seen but rarely heard, stimulating production over which they have no control, becoming consumers of the products that they inspire but do not produce, and finally becoming "consumed"—petted, admired and seduced—by the men who produce for them.

DEVELOPMENTAL SOLUTIONS AND FEMININE STEREOTYPES

Contradictory statements about women in development, some emphasizing their adaptability to change, others showing them as a force of stability, disciplining men, reveal the inadequacy of our constructs for explaining personality, culture, and society in relation to the sex variable. The contradictions stem from a mystique that attributes attitudes to an eternally feminine character and ignores social class and economic factors that condition their responses to change. The United Nations report on women in community development[55] points to some of these factors in the following statement:

> Experts in social development and change have noted that where women's organizations are active, changes are introduced quickly and maintained easily. Women are, on the whole, receptive to change for one explicable reason: they have usually more to gain by changes brought about by community development than by clinging to the *status quo*. It has been observed, however, that rural women, who have frequently shown more desire for innovation and change in this respect than men, often lack the organizations through which to express this desire effectively. In fact, village women's associations, voluntarily set up for social development and welfare are a rare phenomenon in developing countries.

The report indicates that in many countries the role of women in community development was not recognized until recently. Developers continue to defeat the interest and enthusiasm women have shown by casting them in stereotyped roles imported from the developed countries. Many programs, such as the "Better Family Living" projects sponsored by the Food and Agricultural Organization have as their objective "the maintenance of values and functions of home and family living and planning of a happy family life."[55] Even when let out of the home, women are channeled into stereotyped roles, such as stenographers and typists in urban African development projects, nurses and midwives in New Zealand, or mothercraft and homecraft roles through UNICEF.[55] Despite the valuable contribution the United Nations report makes in revealing the status of women in development projects, woven throughout the document are the contradictions implicit in western thought about women's place. Viewing their fundamental responsibility as centered in the home, nutrition, and sewing they advocate letting women into the public domain only after they have completed these basic functions, much as a cow is let out to pasture after being milked.

Frequently women are directed toward voluntary work, whereas men are channeled into paying jobs in the development projects, thus reinforcing the sense that their work is and should be gratuitous. Thus while a United Nations report[56] points to the blocks to women's participation (lack of educational training, vocational guidance and counselling, traditional attitudes of both men and women to roles, and the division of labor in the market), their projects often reinforce rather than do away with the inequality. Boserup has shown[15] how technicians sent in by development agencies are concerned with cash crops where men predominate in the labor force, while women's subsistence crops are rarely considered an important basis for improvement. Cooperatives whose stated aim is to improve the general human welfare succeeded in East Africa in defeating an economically successful crop since men received the money from the harvest their wives produced through their control of the cooperative.[57] Rubbo[58] has shown how the Columbia ICA1 succeeded in breaking down subsistence crops farmed by women in commercial agriculture by urging peasants to cut down the perennial coffee and cocoa trees, replacing them with "green revolution" crops: corn, soya beans, and tomatoes. The new agriculture, which was more "technified" and required the use of fertilizers and machinery, upset the ecology and contributed to single crop cultivation in which the risks are higher. Fals Borda[59] shows, in his review of cooperatives throughout the world, that subsistence crops, which are mainly women's work, are rarely included in the development of cooperatives. When women are included in decision-making positions in cooperatives, their participation is often contingent on their marital status. Alberti[60] states that in Peruvian cooperatives a married woman is subordinate to her husband in the cooperative, but unmarried women may occupy positions of importance.

Mythic reinforcement of feminine stereotypes underwrites the oppression and acceptance of the status quo. As Flora[6] shows, the passivity and other traits attributed to women, Indians, and other lower status figures inhibit the development of ego-strength and adaptive ability to gain conscious control over self and environment. The internalization of the passivity may in part stem from the peculiarity of women's position in the productive process: not only are they producers and consumers, but also they are a product "consumed" by men. Their role, elaborated in the mass media, in courtship and marriage is first to attract by the consumption products they display, accepting male advances without initiating ventures; and if successful in getting a home through marriage, they become a display object validating their husband's success. The inability to act autonomously may also arise from women's sense of their female role as being at odds with what they consider men's ideal women to be, i.e., nurturant, noncompetitive, and passive.[61] Fearful of destroying their relations with men, they avoid revealing their own nature. The male mystique about romance complements this in seeking satisfaction by transcending society rather than by sharing work and risks. This remains a problem in Cuba after the revolution as well as in more tradition-bound societies of Latin American society.[5] Cast as an inspiration, supportive to the male activists, woman is subverted by compliments.

By separating out the differential impact of industrialization on men and women, we can learn about the system as a whole. Assumptions about progress must be assessed along with the economic vulnerability and the political and social dependency cultivated in government, private industry, and international programs of change. We learn to question progress that continues to widen income differentials and crystalizes internal dependencies. We shall pursue this inquiry in the following section.

STRUCTURAL MODELS OF LATIN AMERICAN SOCIETY

The Family

The ideology of the nuclear family as the universal mode of sexual reproduction and socialization of offspring[62] and of the nuclear, patriarchal male-dominated form as the norm in Latin America[63] persists despite the rising frequency of female-headed households. When these occur, they are characterized as matrifocal or even matriarchal, a distortion of the role of women in such circumstances since they bear the economic and social burdens of the reproductive nuclei with none of the rewards of social esteem and economic support given to the males who undertake such responsibilities. Persistence of the stereotype of male-headed families despite the evidence to the contrary makes woman's entry into the labor force a contradiction to her definition of social being, even when she is forced by economic necessity to do so, as Gonzalez[64] shows.

Goode[65] underwrites the ideology of the nuclear family as the bearer of liberation in industrial society, acclaiming the freedom it provides to the individual to choose one's own spouse, freedom from extended kinship constraints, and egalitarianism. He ignores the fundamental constraints imposed on a woman when she loses the support of her kin and is confined to the narrow social sphere of the connubial pair. Lacking the independence that homecrafts or extended kin ties provided in the past, women are forced to choose a spouse not for love, but in consideration of earning power, and they are irrevocably tied to him as increasing offspring limit their ability to enter the labor market.

Taking the family as the unit of sociological investigation, it is commonly assumed that class position is equal for husbands and for wives. Consequently, mobility is assumed to aid both partners, when in fact the woman's movement is dependent on her remaining tied to a male. Mobility for the man, particularly in periods of dynamic economic and political change, is often predicated on abandoning the wife, who was the mate of an impoverished youth, as the man rises in the new positions made available. Even when a woman retains the status of wife, she has few of the attributes of the class position a man enjoys in the exercise of power or even the purchase of privileges. Most government, ecclesiastical, or army positions cannot be acquired by women of any social class, nor can a woman purchase sexual satisfactions or marital stability.

Demographic Structure

The politics of demography in relation to rising populations, falling employment, and a declining death rate have overshadowed the basic human rights involved. Because birth control, planned parenthood programs, and sterilization have been promoted by United States agencies through the Peace Corps, United

States AID, and private business, these programs have been associated with reactionary attempts to subvert people's revolutionary movements. The argument is often made that underdeveloped countries of Latin America are not overpopulated, but have vast undeveloped areas where rising populations can be absorbed. Since these populations are posed as a threat to the aims of control and expropriation by foreign powers in their own interests, the control over births is cast as another expression of imperialist domination. Contradicting the logic of this position, the conservative institutions of the church and state support the same negative position with regard to birth control.

What is not taken into account in either position is the rights women should have to control reproduction in the interest of their own self-determination. Large families inhibit the political effectiveness of the lower classes, particularly in the case of women, thus maintaining conservative and reactionary regimes. Rising population puts an additional burden on Third World countries, which serve, as Selma James[46] points out, as "massive repositories [reproducing] the industrial reserve armies from Port of Spain, Calcutta, Algeria, the Mexican towns of the United States border to the kitchens and bedrooms of the metropolis." At the point when young people become economically active, they are forced to migrate to centers of production, often to the metropolitan centers themselves to find work. The poor populations of the world reproduce and maintain the active labor force until it becomes exploitable to serve in low-paid productive or service jobs. Women experience in their own flesh the tragic consequences of uncontrolled births. When I was conducting research in the mining community of Oruro in Bolivia, I saw women deprive themselves and their female children of protein in the distribution of food, which they gave preferentially to the male breadwinner and to male children. A miner once explained to me that women were in the forefront of the labor struggles in the mines because it is women who have to face their children to tell them that there is nothing to eat, and it is women who have to bear the pain of death from malnourishment or neglect of their children when they are forced to work to help support a large family. The unusual identification of women with class exploitation in the mines stems from the solidarity of the community and the integration of domestic and productive spheres, but it is not without parallels in other working class populations.

Industrialized communities have in some cases lost constraints on population growth that exist in most rural communities. The families may be subsidized by the industrial enterprise, with subsistence allotments after the birth of each child dulling the feedback mechanism which alerts the campesino to the fact that available food supplies might be overtaxed. Furthermore, the herbs used as abortifacients by rural peasants are often unavailable or forgotten, and unless the state or some other agency provides modern equipment at low cost, birth control is neglected.

Education and Occupational Level

In all Latin American countries women have lower literacy levels than men do, and they represent less than half of the population in third-rate educational institutions. However, we cannot conclude that improvement of educational opportunities for women will improve their ability to enter into higher occupational ranges. Educational attainment for all discriminated minorities is a symptom, not a cause of systematic exclusion. In the United States, for example, where a higher percentage of women enter upper-level educational institutions, their professional ratings do not match those of men.[66] Epstein[67] shows that with the enormous increase in higher education from 1910 to 1960, women's participation in professions remained the same or increased only slightly. Academicians remained constant at 19% of the total employed in colleges and universities; women lawyers have increased from 1% to 3.5% of the profession, and doctors from 6 to 6.8%. United States data on comparable income and education for men and women indicate that at each educational level, women earn from less than one-half to no more than three-quarters of what men of comparable education earn, and the overall proportion is 60% of that which men earn.

In Latin America education seems to have a greater effect in overcoming occupational and wage differentials between men and women, but discriminatory channeling of female students still limits their entrance into professional training and limits their participation in the occupations available once they have secured degrees. Jusenius and Finn[68] point to the low enrollment of female students in university courses (one-quarter of the student body) in Ecuador as an index to continued limitation on their participation in the professions in the near future. Data reported by Gonzalez-Salazar[64] for Mexico reveal an improving but still biased situation discriminating against women in education and professional occupations, except those that are an extension of traditional roles in the house such as teaching and nursing.

The plea for greater educational opportunities is a quasisolution for a structural situation that maintains the women in subordination to the male sector of the work force at every level. To attribute discriminatory status to lack of education is to confuse agency with agent. Limitation of entry into education is a means of excluding women from higher statuses; the reason for their exclusion lies in the total social construction of roles. In the lower classes, boys are favored educationally over girls on the assumption that they are more likely to succeed. Even when able to enter universities, women may not do so because they realize they will have little chance to put their professional training into practice. However, although education cannot be posed as a solution, it serves to increase dissatisfaction and thus promote pressure for structural change.

WOMEN'S PERSPECTIVES IN THE SOCIAL SCIENCES

Women social scientists and social commentators are more willing than are men to admit the influence their personal perceptions and empathy with their subjects have in their choice of problems and analyses of data. Flora Tristan,[69] one of the few women commentators of the past century whose words survived in print, reveals the introspection that guided her narrative:

> In the course of my narration, I often speak of myself. I reflect on my sufferings, my thoughts, my affections; all result from the orientation that God has given me, from the education I have received and from the position that the laws and prejudices have made me.

The products of male social commentators are characterized by mastery, ego separation, and enhancement, as Bernard[29] suggests, in contrast to the work of feminine observers. The assumed universality of the male social researcher is underwritten with the identification of humankind with "men."[70] Their questions are posed universalistically, even when their sample is exclusively male. Histories serve to crystallize values that are played out in the selective reference points for thinking about contemporary events. Heroic figures are those who carry out the exploits valued by men and recounted in their history.

We are now in a liminal state in the social sciences as the values on which our selective criteria are premised are being questioned by people who were never before a significant enough part of the professions to challenge them. These include women and natives of the societies studied. Not only do they find the old paradigms wanting, but the very construction of social reality appears based on preconceptions that do not yield to a changing reality. As a consequence of subordination within the profession and in field research, women often develop the kind of double consciousness similar to that of other minorities, an awareness of the motives and strategies of the oppressor as well as the inner view of the oppressed, who must respond constantly to demands made upon them. This awareness is distinct from that of the "stranger" as posed in the sociological literature of the twenties and thirties. It is the view of the insider, aware of the subtleties of discrimination as a second-class participant in the arenas where they are dramatized, ideologized, and reinforced. If we are to develop a social science that is responsive to the needs of the people we study, we must eradicate the dominance hierarchies within the disciplines as well as in the wider society. A participant social science in which the subordinate sectors of society enter into the research and analysis of the conditions that affect their being is one step in that direction.

Appendix

In an attempt to analyze the different perceptions of men and women in research, we sent a questionnaire to men and women who have recently done field work in Latin America. The responses suggest that the self-image of male research is less fraught with ambiguities and contradictions which threaten the role as sensed by female researchers. While both men and women respondents indicated an awareness of sex stereotyping while doing research (fifteen of seventeen women and nine of thirteen men) only one of the male respondents felt that he was excluded from events because of his sex while twelve women felt that they were barred from significant participation at various levels. The kinds of events women listed included "serious talks with male community leaders," political meetings, religious brotherhoods, night drinking and other social activities except with an escort, and entering mine pits. Only one male respondent listed a specific event: baby showers. Five men qualified their response, saying that they were not excluded from any events of importance. While women consider all-male activities to be of importance, most males take it for granted that all women's groups are trivial. Women reported trying to overcome sex stereotyping by emphasizing their professional status in five cases, their upper class identity or status as a foreigner, or reclassifying themselves as "men" by their behavior. Men, when they noted sex stereotyping in the reaction of associates, claimed to enjoy it (in one case), ignore it (in four cases), or conform to tradition (one case).

Some of the most interesting comments were in response to an open-ended question, "Do you feel that your socialization into the profession has influenced your sexual perspective and your approach to the study of social relations in any particular way?" Among male comments deserving note is the following.

> Yes, I have become less a sexist, and have grown away from a stereotypical view of women academics. I now appreciate my female colleagues for their skills

and for their special perspective on some important sociological issues, e.g. socialization. (*From a sociologist.*)

Women were more responsive to this question, as well as to other open-ended questions and did not seem to have as much difficulty in interpreting questions on sexual perspective. Among some of the more interesting comments are the following:

> * Yes, in very definite ways. Having been in close association with a woman professor in anthropology who has been very active in women's studies has awakened my interest in the field. Having acquired an "anthropological" or cross-cultural perspective on women has influenced not only my personal sexual perspective, but my professional one as well. I have become sensitized to the traditional and sometimes subtle male-orientation of the perception and analysis of social relations in anthropology (e.g., kinship). Finally, as a Latin American woman trying to do field work and establish myself professionally in Latin America, I have had experiences which have had repercussions on my perspective and approach as a female in my profession.
>
> * Yes, dealing with some men who are extremely prejudiced against women as professionals has made me much more conscious that we are not yet to the stage where I'd supposed, [where] we can all *be* professional, as economists, without considering sex.
>
> * Recently, yes; new attitudes toward women have determined some choices of research topics; I am particularly interested in types of explanations, variations, etc. in female political participation of "lower" participation; general impression that women can be more accepted in political as well as professional roles in Latin America than in U.S. until recently.
>
> * Very much so. It was something I really had to overcome while doing my dissertation, which was on Pentecostals and social change in Colombia. It took a lot of consciousness raising for me to feel that women could somehow be actors in social change. I almost left them out of my study entirely, except that I had much better rapport with Colombian women than Colombian men, and I felt more at ease with them.
>
> * I am keenly aware of the problems of women at many levels, the limited boundaries within which they have had to function in the past and the many attitudinal changes which are still necessary to make them realize their potential fully. I am particularly aware of the problems of the middle-aged woman who wishes to pursue a career, since I was 34 when I began my graduate work. I feel that there is a subtle discrimination against individuals past a certain age in the job market, and particularly toward women interested in obtaining a permanent long-term position. I graduated in August of 1973. I have been unable to obtain a position in my field and at present I am teaching in junior high. There is an unspoken attitude among many of the males with whom I spoke either while doing my research or applying for a job that women do not take their work seriously, and that they do not have the aggressiveness and endurance necessary to pursue a full-time career. There is an "old boys' club" among the faculties of many institutions of higher learning, and only enforcement of hiring quotas will open some departments to more women.

The respondents indicate in their remarks not only a growing personal awareness of the influence sex role perspective has on their work, but also the increasing sensitivity in their fields. Women have had to come to terms with the problem because restrictions on their entry into the profession or into research activities have forced it on their consciousness. As yet most men have been only subliminally aware, and even enjoy the advantages sex role stereotyping seems to allow them.

However, as the first sociologist quoted above indicates, men as well as women can gain sensitivity to social issues by becoming aware of people's stereotypes about them and their own preconceptions about others.

REFERENCES

1. CHANEY, E. 1973. Old and new feminists in Latin America: The case of Peru and Chile, J. Marr. Family **35** (2): 331–43.
2. GUEILER TEJADA, L. 1959. La Mujer y la Revolución. La Paz, Bolivia.
3. JAQUETTE, J. 1974. Women in Politics. John Wiley. New York, N.Y.
4. NASH, J. 1975. Women in resistance movements in Bolivia. *In* Women Cross Culturally: Change and Challenge. R. Leavitt, Ed. Mouton. The Hague, The Netherlands.
5. TURNER, F. C. 1967. Los efectos de la participacion feminina en la revolucion de 1910. Historia Mexicana **16**: 602–20.
6. FLORA BUTLER, C. 1971. The passive female: Her comparative image by class and culture in women's magazine fiction. J. Marr. Family **33**: 000–000.
7. PESCATELLO, A. 1973. Female and Male in Latin America; Essays. University of Pittsburgh Press. Pittsburgh, Pa.
8. CHINAS, B. 1973. The Zapotec Women. Holt, Rhinhart, and Winston. New York, N.Y.
9. ELMENDORF, M. L. 1972. The Mayan Woman and Change. Ph.D. thesis, Union Graduate School.
10. HELBLOM, A.-B. 1967. La participación cultural de las mujeres: Indias y mestizas en el México precortesiano y postrevolucionario. Etnografiska Museet. Stockholm, Sweden.
11. SHAPIRO, J. 1972. Sex Roles and Social Structure among the Yanomama Indians of Northern Brazil. Unpublished Ph.D. thesis, Columbia University.
12. GOODALE, J. C. 1971. Tiwi Wives: A Study of Women of Melville Island, No. Australia. University of Washington Press. Seattle, Washington.
13. KAYBERRY, P. M. 1939. Aboriginal Woman, Sacred and Profane. Routledge and Sons, Ltd. London, England.
14. AGUIAR, N. The impact of industrialization on women's work roles in the northeast of Brazil. *In* Sex and Class in Latin America. J. Nash and H. Sofa, Eds. Praeger. New York, N.Y. To be published.
15. BOSERUP, E. 1970. Women's Role in Economic Development. Allen and Unwin. London, England.
16. HARKNESS, S. J. 1973. The pursuit of an ideal: Migration, social class and women's roles in Bogota, Colombia. *In* Female and Male in Latin America. A. Pescatello, Ed. University of Pittsburgh Press. Pittsburgh, Pa.
17. RIBEIRO, L. & M. TERESITA DE BARBIERE. 1973. La mujer obrera chilena: una aproximación a su estudio. Cuadernos de la Realidad Nacional **16**: 167–202.
18. SAFFIOTI, H. I. B. 1969. A Mulher na Sociedade de Classe: Mito e Realidade. Quatro Artes. Sao Paulo, Brazil.
19. MADDEN, J. 1973. The Economics of Sex Discrimination. Lexington Books. Lexington, Mass.
20. SMITH, M. 1973. Domestic service as a channel for upward mobility: the Lima Case. *In* Pescatello, *op. cit.*: 197–201.
21. DALLA COSTA, M. & S. JAMES. 1972. Women and the subversion of the community. *In* The Power of Women and the Subversion of the Community. The Falling Wall Press. Bristol.
22. NASH, J. Dependency and the failure of feedback: The case of Bolivian mining communities. *In* Proceedings of the XLVth International Congress of Latin Americanists, Vol. 30. Tilgher Press. Rome, Italy.
23. DE VRIES, E. & J. MEDINA ECHAVARRIA. 1960. Social Aspects of Economic Development in Latin America. Vol. 1. UNESCO.
24. INKELES, A. 1969. Making men modern: On the causes and consequences of individual change in six developing countries. Amer. J. Sociol. **75**: 208–225.
25. KAHL, J. 1968. The Measurement of Modernism: A Study of Values in Brazil and Mexico. University of Texas Press. Austin, Texas.
26. ARDNER, S. 1973. Sexual insult and female militancy. Man **8** (3): 422–40.
27. LA FONTAINE, J. 1972. Ritualization of women's life crisis in Bugisu. *In* The Inter-

pretation of Ritual: Essays in Honour of A. I. Richards. Tavistock. London, England.
28. LEAVITT, R.R., B. SYKES & E. WEATHERFORD. 1972. Aboriginal woman: Male and female anthropological perspectives. Presented at the 1972 meeting of the American Anthropological Association.
29. BERNARD, J. 1973. My four revolutions: An autobiographical history of the American Sociological Association. Amer. J. Sociol. **78** (5): 739–91.
30. VEKEMANS, R. & J. L. SEGUNDO. 1963. Essay on a socio-economic typology of the Latin American Countries. *In* Social Aspects of Economic Development in Latin America. E. de Vries and J. Medina Echavarria, Eds. UNESCO.
31. LEACOCK, E. 1972. Introduction. *In* The Origin of the Family, Private Property and the State in the Light of the Researches of Lewis H. Morgan, by Frederick Engels. International Publications. New York, N.Y.
32. LERNER, D. 1964. The Passing of Traditional Society; Modernizing the Middle East.: 4. Free Press. New York, N.Y.
33. LERNER, D. *Ibid.*: 204.
34. ROSEN, B. C. & A. L. LA RAIA. 1972. Modernity in women: An Index of social change in Brazil. J. Marr. Family **34**: 353–360.
35. WERTHEIM, W. F. 1964. East-West Parallels: Sociological Approaches to Modern Asia. Quadrangle Press. Chicago, Ill.
36. DEUTSCH, K. 1961. Social mobilization and political development. American Political Science Review LVI: 463–515. (Quoted in Eisenstadt.)
37. EISENSTADT, S. N. 1966. Modernization, growth and diversity. America Latina **9**: 34–58.
38. GANS, M., J. PASTORE & E. A. WILKENING. 1970. A mulher e a modernizacão da familia brasilera. Pesquish o planejamento **12** (Oct.): 97–139.
39. WEINER, M. 1966. Modernization: The Dynamics of Growth. Basic Books. New York, N.Y.
40. WOOD, R. 1966. The future of modernization. *In* Weiner, *op. cit.*: 40–54.
41. MITCHELL, J. 1971. Woman's Estate. Pantheon Books. New York, N.Y.
42. MATTELART, M. 1970. El nivel mitico en la prensa seudoamorosa. Cuadernos de la Realidad Nacional **3**: 221–34.
43. United National Economic Commission for Latin America (ECLA). 1970. Development Problems in Latin Ameria. University of Texas Press. Austin, Texas.
44. DESANTI, D. 1972. Flora Tristan, la Femme Revolte. Hachette. Paris, France.
45. LARGIA, I. & J. DEMOULIN. 1972. Toward a science of women's liberation. NACLA's Latin America and Empire Report. VI (10).
46. JAMES, S. 1973. Sex, race and working class power. Race Today (January).
47. JELIN, E. n.d. La Bahiana en la fuerza de trabajo: Actividad domestica, produccion simple y trabajo asalariado en Salvador, Bahia. Presented at the Conference on Feminine Perspectives in Latin America, Buenos Aires, March, 1974.
48. SCHWENDINGERS, J. & H. SCHWENDINGERS. 1971. Sociology's founding fathers: Sexists to a man. J. Marr. Family **33**: 783–799.
49. WARD, L. I. 1883. Dynamic Sociology. Appleton and Co. New York, N.Y.
50. THOMAS, W. I. 1907. Sex and Society. The Gorham Press. Boston, Mass.
51. LEWIS, O. 1966. The culture of poverty. Scientific American **215**: 19–25.
52. NUN, J. 1969. Superpoblación relativa al ejercito industrial de reserva y masa marginal. Instituto di Tella. Buenos Aires, Argentina.
53. CAMARANO, C. 1971. On Cuban women. *In* Liberation Now.: 364–76. Dell Publishing Co. New York, N.Y.
54. OLESON, V. 1971. Context and Posture: Notes on Socio Cultural Aspects of Women's Roles and Family Policy in Contemporary Cuba. J. Marr. Family **33**: 548–60.
55. United Nations Commission on the Status of Women. 1972. Participation of Women in Community Development.
56. United Nations Commission on the Status of Women. 1970. Participation of Women in the Economic and Social Development of their Countries. New York, N.Y.
57. APTHORPE, R. J. 1970. Some problems of evaluation. *In* Co-operatives and Rural Development in East Africa. C. G. Widstrand, Ed.: 209–229. Africana Publishing Corp. New York, N.Y.
58. RUBBO, A. n.d. The spread of rural capitalism—its effects on black women in the Cauca Valley, Western Colombia. Estudios Andinos. To be published.
59. FALS BORDA, O. 1972. El Reformismo por Dentro en America Latina. Siglo XXI. Mexico.
60. ALBERTI. Personal communication.

61. STEINMANN, A. & D. J. FOX. 1969. Specific areas of agreement and conflict in women's self-perception and their perception of men's ideal woman in two Southamerican communities and an urban community in the United States. J. Marr. Family 31 (2): 281–9.
62. MURDOCK, G. P. 1949. Social Structure. Macmillan Co. New York, N.Y.
63. CARLOS, M. L. & L. SELLERS. 1972. Family, kinship structure and modernization in Latin America. Latin American Research Review VII (2): 95–124.
64. GONZALEZ-SALAZAR, G. n.d. La participación de la mujer en la actividad laboral de Mexico. *In* Sex and Class in Latin America. J. Nash and H. Sofa, Eds. Praeger. New York, N.Y.
65. GOODE, W. J. 1963. World Revolution and Family Patterns. Free Press. New York, N.Y.
66. OPPENHEIMER, V. X. 1972. Rising educational attainment, declining fertility and the inadequacies of the female labor market. *In* Commission of Population Growth and the American Future.
67. EPSTEIN, C. F. 1970. Woman's Place: Options and Limits in Professional Careers. University of California Press. Berkeley, Calif.
68. JUSENIUS, C. & M. FINN. n.d. The position of women in the Ecuadorian economy. Estudios Andinos. To be published.
69. TRISTAN Y MOSCOZO, F. 1959. Peregrinaciones de una Paria: Seleccion Portico y Notas de Catalina Recavarren de Zizold. Ed. Tierra Nueva. Lima, Peru.
70. ELU DE LENERO, M. C. n.d. Perspectivas femininas sobre la investigacion de ciencias sociales en America Latina: Esterotipo y realidad. *In* Sex and Class in Latin America. J. Nash and H. Sofa, Eds. Praeger. New York, N.Y.
71. GERMANI.

THE ROLE OF THE AMERICAN CHEMICAL SOCIETY RE SCIENCE PUBLIC POLICY

Bernard S. Friedman

American Chemical Society
Washington, D.C. 20036

Two years hence, in 1976, our Nation will celebrate the 200th anniversary of its founding. That year will mark another anniversary—the 100th year after the founding of the American Chemical Society.

In its early years the ACS did little thinking about public affairs and political decisions; nor did it pay much attention to the adverse or potentially adverse side effects of chemical technology. It concentrated on the traditional activities of a learned society: the development and dissemination of scientific information, mainly to practitioners and future practitioners. True, there was some interest in public affairs; the ACS did take an active role in protecting the public against harmful food additives, and lent assistance to the Chemical Warfare Branch of the Department of the Army.

However, in its 61st year, back in 1937, the ACS was granted a national charter by the United States Congress which placed a responsibility and obligation on the Society to provide technical advice and investigative assistance to the federal government on public issues and problems.

In recent decades legislators and government officials have become aware that research discoveries and developments play a dominant role in our economy, foreign trade balance, and employment. They began to realize that our material resources, energy and conservation, our health, nutrition, and environment, and the quality of our life are affected by scientific research and development.

There was an obvious need, however, for chemical scientists to do what they could to increase this awareness on the part of our legislators and officials, to sharpen and clarify their understanding of how science and technology operate, and to provide them with an insight into the process by which basic or exploratory discoveries are translated into practical outcomes for the benefit of the nation, its people—the world and *its* people.

At the same time it was also necessary to ensure that our own members were fully aware that Congress, the Executive Branch, and the judicial system were evolving legislation, regulations and decisions that vitally and directly (1) affected the way chemical scientists are trained (scholarships and fellowships, grants for laboratories, equipment, and libraries); (2) affected the way their products are manufactured, marketed, or used (patents and copyright laws; health, safety, environmental, consumer as well as chemical warfare policies or regulations); (3) affected the availability of their raw materials, power, and fuel ; (4) affected their professional relations (pensions, patents, antidiscrimination measures, immigration preference quotas and government conclusions re supply and demand for chemists); and (5) affected the support of fundamental research.

The question had to be faced: What was the best way to make sure the policy-makers in government would have the correct and pertinent scientific facts at their disposal? And to what extent should the ACS and its sister societies try to influence the decision-making process?

About ten years ago the Society established a Committee to provide coordination of the Society's activities in the area of Chemistry and Public Affairs (CCPA). Under the dynamic leadership in turn of Charles C. Price, Franklin A. Long, and Charles G. Overberger—and with the assistance of its members, most of whom are nationally-known, knowledgeable experts—the Committee has become increasingly active and effective in helping the Society to respond to the public need.

The Committee has sponsored many symposia at our national meetings to educate our own members on issues in public and government affairs. It published a report, *Cleaning our Environment—The Chemical Basis for Action,* which is now in its seventh printing. Undoubtedly this report was of benefit to congressmen (who were all supplied copies) in preparing legislation on pollution and ecology.

The Committee recently issued *Chemistry in the Economy,* a comprehensive study showing the pervasive character of chemistry in almost all branches of our economy. *Chemistry in Medicine* will soon appear.

Admittedly such activities are low-profile, but these in-depth studies on problems of national urgency are major contributions to the understanding and ultimate solution of these problems. Over the years, however, CCPA has developed a more active posture for the ACS, resulting in more direct interaction with those in the political decision-making arena.

To be effective, the Society needed to be alert and informed. We soon found that the tasks of monitoring the three branches of the Government, maintaining liaison with government officials, summarizing the information for distribution to our members, and the preparation of position papers, could not be satisfactorily handled by volunteer members, but would require full-time, salaried, competent, knowledgeable staff. A new department, the Department of Chemistry and Public Affairs, was established in 1966 to handle these tasks. It now has a staff of four professionals (all with doctorates in chemistry) and the necessary support personnel.

Headed by talented and experienced Dr. Stephen T. Quigley, the Department alerts ACS Committees, the Board of Directors, officers, and staff regarding federal activities involving chemistry and science public policy. When it is recognized that ACS input would be highly desirable regarding a given item, steps are taken by the Department to get the recommendations of the appropriate ACS groups and persons. These recommendations furnish the basis for a rough-draft statement (if one seems warranted) of the position the Society might take. The rough draft is then circulated for review and revision. The final draft is then presented to the Board for approval. When it is approved, Dr. Quigley arranges for the Society to be invited to present testimony. This is usually given by the Society president; however, when the occasion or subject warrants, one of the other officers (or committee chairmen) will make the presentation.

In recent years official statements have been presented in testimony before congressional committees on such diverse topics as the Geneva Protocol on Chemical Warfare, pension reform, patent and copyright reform, the development and integration of science information systems across discipline boundaries, and federal science and technology policy (including provisions for manpower impact statement). Among the measures proposed: a high-level Council and/or cabinet-level department of science and technology; emergency Occupational Safety and Health Administration (OSHA) standards for work on certain carcinogens and other hazardous materials. Our testimony has covered specifics such as mechanisms for the effective management of the country's technology policy, and surveys of the nation's technological resources and applications.

A new study, *Energy and the Environment—The Chemical Viewpoint,* being prepared under the supervision of CCPA is expected to have a strong impact on legislation.

The usual pattern has been for the ACS to react to some crisis (such as the energy crisis) or to respond only on request for comment on proposed legislation, but this is changing. For example, a subcommittee chaired by Dr. Richard W. Roberts, Director of the Bureau of Standards, is now investigating vital materials resources in order to develop *in advance* information and recommendations to enable the nation to cope with a potential crisis in this area.

As a further step in developing more active membership involvement in exercising the Society's Charter responsibilities, CCPA has developed what we call the "Congressional Science Advisor" program. In this program, ACS members have been designated to serve on a one-to-one basis each as counselor or advisor to his Representative or Senator. Since the Science Advisor will be a constituent of the individual congressman, the relationship should make for such easier contact and greater rapport between them. Each Advisor will, within the scope of his own scientific and technology competence, offer to help the congressman and his staff on any legislative problem involving chemistry. If the Advisor is not able to supply the information needed, he or she can call upon one or more of the ACS specialized committees for assistance.

Many congressmen have recognized the need for scientific advice and indeed have told the ACS that it should be more active and timely in offering such advice.

Dr. William J. Bailey is giving this program leadership, and he expects to give it lots of attention and support during his term as the 1975 ACS President.

At the present time, enough volunteers are lined up to furnish a Science Advisor for practically every member of Congress.

Incidentally, the Science Advisors consider themselves as official ACS spokesmen only when they are transmitting and/or interpreting Board-approved policy statements.

What I've described are efforts designed to have an impact on current or near-future governmental actions and policy. But for the long-range we most certainly need to improve the understanding and awareness of the public as to how science and technology have affected and will affect the lives of all. To me that means that all students should have courses in Chemistry and/or the other physical and biological sciences. Adults should be made aware through radio, TV, easy-to-read books, visual aids, science lectures and panels, and courses.

Better informed citizens would lead to the selection of public servants and legislators more knowledgeable about science and technology. A better-informed public would be willing to encourage congressmen and officials to support needed R & D and to supply funds needed to upgrade teaching and training in these fields.

Many of these programs would have a better chance of succeeding if they were sponsored by joint action of the nation's scientific and technological societies. We have made a good start in this direction, thanks largely to the vision and efforts of Dr. Alan C. Nixon, the 1973 ACS President. With the encouragement of the ACS Board and Council, Dr. Nixon brought together scientific society presidents (initially 20, now 33) to form the Committee of Scientific Society Presidents (CSSP) for the purpose of exchanging information and discussing joint recommendations in many areas including public and government relations.

Earlier this year (January 22) Dr. Nixon with aid of ACS staff was able to arrange a luncheon meeting of the CSSP with Gerald Ford, who was Vice-President at the time. Thirty representatives of 23 societies were present and joined in frank, friendly exchange of views and suggestions with Mr. Ford. He in turn responded to questions in an open, thoughtful, and encouraging manner—and asked questions, posed problems, and explored solutions with us. On October 9 the Committee had an equally informative and stimulating luncheon meeting with Senator Edward Kennedy. The CSSP thought these exchanges most useful, and plans to follow them up with similar meetings with other congressional leaders, and on occasion with their top staff.

In addition, Dr. Nixon has been very effective in maintaining liaison with CCESP, the Coordinating Committee of Engineering Society Presidents. CCESP is also active in developing and communicating public policy positions.

It is obvious that in formulating and expressing the views of its members regarding science public policies, the ACS is operating as a representative democracy. Constraints of time and geography make it unfeasible if not impossible to involve the 105,000 members-at-large in this process. Those who are directly involved, however, are determined that the official stands of the ACS shall represent the best judgment of the chemical scientific and technical community, and that these stands could with some degree of confidence be said to represent the consensus of all its members. Consensus cannot be easy for a membership such as ours, reflecting as it does a broad range of engagement (60% in industry,* 25% in academia, and 15% in government and nonprofit institutions). The members are kept well-informed of ACS science public policy actions through reports in *Chemical and Engineering News*, the ACS weekly magazine.

How effective is the Society's imput? This, of course, is often impossible to quantify, but we are pleased to report that our position papers and statements and testimony are accorded respectful attention and earn frequent expressions of appreciation. This may be due to the fact that our messages are recognized as the group expression of our 105,000 members—and that our positions are based on a thorough and thoughtful consideration by a broad spectrum of knowledgeable chemical scientists and technologists. We make every attempt to ensure that our recommendations are sound and judicious, as free as humanly possible from institutional or professional bias, and that the public weal is kept paramount.

Probably important is the fact that our presentations are low-key and thoughtful. To maintain credibility we avoid overdoing our bit, and are careful not to give the impression that we want "in" on every act. Nothing turns off a congressman or legislator as much as the constituent who grabs his lapel too frequently.

We have been encouraged by the number of occasions when actions taken by congressional committees or federal agencies comported with our recommendations. For example, four of five of our recommendations were adopted in connection with the Toxic Substances Control Act. All the recommendations of the Society were incorporated into H.R.2, the Pension Reform Bill.

It is also encouraging to note that stands taken by our sister societies, individually or jointly, very frequently coincide with those of the ACS. Thus we feel that our voice, individual or collective, is bound to have a salutary effect, contributing to the progress of science and the well-being of our profession and that of the public.

In summary, it seems that the "pure" learned society is a thing of the past. It makes no sense for us scientists and engineers (and our associations) to remain aloof, hesitating to take stands re science public policy decisions and regulations. In no way can we escape the effect—good or bad—of government actions or inaction. Fortunately, we have recognized the need, opportunity and challenge, and have accepted the responsibility of getting into the act.

---

* Membership open only to individual chemists; we have no corporate memberships.

GENERAL DISCUSSION

DR. VERA RUBIN: My first free association with Dr. Friedman's last comment is the famous remark "What's good for General Motors is good for the country." I'm not sure that what's good for the professions is necessarily good for the public welfare, but maybe a meeting like this can begin to establish some common ground for discussion.

I want to start with the seemingly simple comment that all of us, elite scientists as well as elite funders, are part of our society. We have to remember that no matter how objective we consider our work to be, it's not only part of the social, cultural, and political framework within which we live, but is also part of a *Zeitgeist*, and the research as well as the funding reflects those factors.

These days, of course, the directions of research are affected by the vagaries of both congressional and foundation funding. This has been instrumental in directing and conditioning research for the past 30 years.

As Dr. Friedman noted, there was little funding of this kind before World War II. Most research was done through private means; fortunately or unfortunately the huge grants that we have become accustomed to were not available. World War II was a watershed in support of social science research as well as the so-called hard sciences.

The Office of Naval Research even supported anthropology during World War II. Some very important studies came out of those initial grants, and I want to mention only one since Dr. Weltfish is here, and that was the work on race, which was done mainly by anthropologists during this period. Dr. Weltfish and Dr. Ruth Benedict were responsible for some of our basic scientific statements about race. World War II, as some of us remember, was a popular war, and scientists were committed to national goals as well as to the furtherance of their own research.

I want to comment on Dr. Creutz's paper, and that is to emphasize the shadow of Congress that lurks over all federal funding, and again is reflected in foundation funding. You're all aware of congressmen who frequently ridicule seemingly foolish or irrelevant research projects that have been funded, as an excuse for cuts in federal appropriations. The political climate affects levels of federal support for international research as well as it does for research in this country.

The problem of elitism that was very interestingly parried between Dr. Rose and Dr. Creutz is not really a question, in terms of funding, about whether scientists constitute an elite group because they are by definition; it's a descriptive social classification of the species *Homo scientificus*.

The question of peer-review committees, however, is another problem. It isn't simply that there are "8,000 elite people" who are drawn upon to determine whether or not research is to be funded or not, but that there is a tendency for the composition of the review committees to become stratified elites who support old school ties in the evaluation of research priorities.

The point that Dr. Rose, our overseas panelist, raised about the "sexist, elitist, and racist" orientation of United States science, I think affects us here primarily in terms of the affirmative action questions. Those of us who are involved in overseas research need to be aware that the rest of the world tends to view United States support of studies abroad as chauvinistic, and our alleged scientific imperialism as a new form of colonialism. Whether we agree or disagree with this viewpoint, it's a social reality that we have to deal with. This view is due partly to the academic brain drain, where the affluent United States has been able to draw scientists from other countries—and this has particularly serious consequences for countries that have a limited academic elite—not only with salary increases but also with research opportunities. Another point of tension in international research is the feeling held by many academics in so-called lesser-developed countries that the attitude of American scientists is arrogant toward their overseas colleagues. They feel that the American scientists do not treat them as peers, fail to exchange data that they have accumulated in those countries or to send reports in the language of the country, and extract research data that is now regarded as a national resource, just as archeological finds are regarded as a national resource. Many countries, particularly ones in the Western hemisphere that have pre-Columbian artifacts, have recently passed stringent laws about the removal of these finds, which are irreplaceable. "Third world" social scientists are beginning to look on research data the same way: They are a national resource that American scientists are taking without providing any reciprocal academic benefits.

Whether we're in the foundation business or in the grantsmanship business, we all know the currently fashionable topics for research: drugs, population, cancer, heart. Sometimes the allocation of funds is not just a question of the public welfare, but of public relations or the concern of a particular administration or president. It becomes a question of grantsmanship, so that the skillful grantsman can work out a proposal that covers his particular interest as well as the national options available in funding. And a skillful reviewer can see that the grantee really wants to do X, but is including Y in order to get the grant. If he's a compassionate reviewer he'll go along with it, but that doesn't always happen.

I do feel, however, that the dichotomy between basic and applied research is a false one that applied research, which is presumably what the country is funding now, has to stem from basic data. You cannot do applied research unless you have the basic data on which to build your research design. And, furthermore, good applied research throws off hypotheses for so-called basic research. There's a complete intertwining of the two lines of research that goes from anthropology to physics to zoology.

Much of the funding for special studies helps to support academic institutions through overhead and indirect provision for other research as well as administrative costs. This has become a recognized if somewhat hidden way of supporting such institutions as universities and medical faculties. However, as Dr. Roth pointed out, there is a devastating effect of cuts in research, which then not only curtails the particular research project that has been funded, but all the supporting services that are needed to carry out that and other research. This is even more critical in the area of overseas grants for fewer foreign universities or institutions are in a position to support the same level of research once the grant has been curtailed. Overseas universities have been concerned about the economic precedents set by grants from the United States which they may not be able to maintain. However, since a good deal of overseas research is now being curtailed, this problem of maintaining "soft money" standards will probably not be as serious as it has been in the recent past.

Dr. Roth raised an interesting question about the problems of academia in national policy-making. It is my strong feeling that because of the increased availability of funding over the past thirty years, academia tends to be receptive rather than active in the situation: they go where the bread is. It's an ad hoc situation as a reality factor; for one thing, academics have practically no voice in real policy-making. Whether that's a passive or reactive situation and whether academia has tried in any constructive or serious way to become involved in policy making is a matter for some study. The White House science advisory apparatus that was dismantled during the Nixon administration is still to be reorganized. It will be interesting to see what impact scientists may have on basic national issues in the future.

The interesting paper by Dr. Nash, which deserves much more discussion than I can give it as present, reflects one of the elements of the *Zeitgeist* with which we are all becoming concerned, and that is the current euphemism of "affirmative action." This is not just a question of research models. Affirmative action is raising the consciousness, if I may use another laden term, of the university community about questions of double standards in academic appointments, academic promotions, and distribution of research grants as well as in the design of particular research models. This may not be a universal problem of research models. I am working mainly in the area of Caribbean studies, where a particular form of family organization has been described as matrifocal. Most social science research for the last twenty years has concerned itself with this so-called matrifocal family. There is now beginning to be an undercurrent of protest that the concerns about matrifocality are leaving the males in a sociological limbo; the last book that's come out on this subject talks about the obsession of social scientists with matrifocality to the total exclusion of patrifocality.

The time has come when we should be concerned about social interaction without particular emphasis on one sex, or one group, or one sector of society, although I recognize that it's necessary to bring to our attention that there has been and still is discrimination based on sex in the social sciences.

Dr. Nash's paper reminded me of the familiar expression, "never underestimate the power of a woman." This was coined by an Italian male who was overwhelmed by the spending power of American women. He felt that women's role in consumerism was a very salient factor in the development of the whole economy, whether or not it is recognized on that basis.

I will make a final comment about the role of scientists themselves in dealing with the current crisis in terms of funding, and the perhaps even deeper crisis in terms of research orientation. Given the complexity of our research interests and the essentially elitist professional tendencies to individualism, which are hard to erase despite the current emphasis on group research and the general fragmentation of research specialties, it occurs to me that perhaps we are really *lumpen* professionals. We have neither a general organizational base nor broad universal goals aside from those of fulfilling a particular research commitment. We certainly have no power. I'm not sure whether the proposed committee of professional presidents is a solution to this problem; but we're in a very serious position now both in terms of the flood of available research, which no one individual can any longer master, and the general lack of direction in research. As we have to determine whether what is good for General Motors is good for the country, so too we have to determine whether what is good for the research community is good for the public welfare, and we must try to find some meeting ground that will make sense in the troubled years to come.

DR. FRIEDMAN: I'm so glad you ended on that note—that there should be a balance about what is good for the profession and what is good for the society-at-large and government—because you started by singling out the single remark of my whole talk which seemed to deny this philosophy.

DR. RUBIN: I'm aware of that, but as I said, it was a free association.

DR. FRIEDMAN: I hope you will carry away with you the other remarks I made about how the American Chemical Society does its best to ensure that any presentation it makes must give the highest priority to the public welfare. This is the remark I want you to remember, not the other one.

BILL BENNETT (*Los Alamos, N. M.*): I would like to defend the context of my earlier remark that emphasized a distinction between basic research and applied research. When those reviews and decisions for funding are being made they are necessarily with respect to certain national goals. I believe that we are in great danger from the centralization of that power since we find it necessary to respond to measures of effectiveness in the OMB. The current permutation of those initials is MBO, Management by Objective, the new "in" term for this sort of thing! Unless we attempt to make some allocation to research that does not necessarily have any applied objective, this research will be neglected. Those who are worthy of support can best be recognized by the people who are working closely with them, which is why I talked about allocation of discretionary funds to the director of a laboratory, for example.

I was very gratified by Dr. Friedman's remarks and at the program of the ACS and the other societies in providing scientific advice to the Congress.

In speaking to us one time at Los Alamos, Congressman Mike McCormack, who is also a chemist, made the point that his colleagues were lawyers and that they didn't understand what he was talking about. When he tried to remind them of the laws of thermodynamics, their immediate response was that surely you could find a way around them!

DR. SIEKEVITZ: I'd like to remind everyone here that through the efforts of Dr. Friedman and Alan Nixon the program of the ACS has become almost revolutionary compared to the way it was. However, Dr. Friedman, although you spoke of the machinery of the ACS's interaction with the legislative body, you didn't mention the *contents* of the advice. Also, most of your members are industrial chemists. How do they feel about what's happening within the ACS in the last three or four years? Do you feel themselves to be part of the lumpenproletariat? Are they going to do anything about this through the ACS? Is the directorship and membership of the ACS trying to educate the members of the ACS as to their role as scientists and workers in an industrial establishment?

DR. FRIEDMAN: Yes, but instead of listing what we have presented to congressional committees and federal officials I would refer you to the abstract of my talk.

We have to educate our members. We do it partly by means of our candidates' statements and platforms; each of us has been elected on the basis of what we wrote and promised. (I hope they don't hold me to all my promises!)

The members are getting a good strong feeling of what the ACS is up to now. They may not be fully supportive, but at least they are permissive. We will arrive at the state of full support gradually, I suppose. The process of education has to start at high school and college levels. Too much of the chemistry taught consists of mathematical equations and theory. Too often the instructor doesn't mention the ramifications of science in our present day society, and its responsibilities and adverse effects. The fact is human beings are seldom mentioned in the text books or in the lecture. I've been jaw-boning about that and I expect to make some impact. There is a trend now away from chemical-bonds approach, and more emphasis on the interaction between science and society, particularly in the courses meant for nonchemists. I'm strongly advocating that trend. It was one of my major platform objectives; I hope we'll make some progress.

We have to educate the public; otherwise we won't get congressmen who know about chemistry or who even want to understand its role in our civilization.

(Every time I say the word chemistry, please feel free to substitute the word science.) Most congressmen want to understand science, but many are not equipped to do that. The people elected by the public aren't going to be scientists, unless the public realizes that their legislators must understand science. That won't happen until the public itself understands something about the role of science and how it will affect our future and the quality of life. The whole process really begins in the schools.

LESTER TALKINGTON: Dr. Friedman, it seems to me that this committee of scientific societies could bypass the top figures of the public and try to reach us through more basic levels, such as the labor movement. A conference of scientific societies with labor representatives might set up a dialogue with fruitful results.

Dr. Nash, I agree with every one of your condemnations of the effects of capitalism both here and abroad on the status of women and the relations between the sexes. However, you offered no program beyond trying to reorient the method of scientific investigation. But in Cuba much of significance is happening with respect to the status of women. An active program has been undertaken there to bring women into the production forces, and it is succeeding. The movement was slow at first, but is more rapid now, and the attack has been legal, economic, and moral. The literature and the movies are very strong in combating *machismo*. Scientists should consider the socialist resolution in designing their studies and in weighing alternatives.

DR. MILLER: Dr. Roth, is there any way in which the universities can resist becoming problem-solvers for the government and still remain recipients of funds to carry out the research that belongs in the Academy? I believe you said that the universities are resisting the use of funds for immediate applied research, but I don't know what the outcome of that resistance is.

DR. ROTH: I'm not sure that I said that they are resisting, but rather that they should resist. There is a movement to try to push institutions of higher education toward the role of problem-solver, which in my view is neither proper to, nor consistent with, academic research. I believe the New York Academy of Sciences can perform a profound service by helping, through conferences such as this, to develop a set of guidelines for appropriate academic research. What are its goals and its limitations with respect to the society at large?

In my view, one I believe shared by many people, the only kind of research activity for which higher education is fitted is that clearly allied to the educational programs of a given college or university. There needn't be an immediate linkage, but at least some recognizable global relationships should exist that hopefully can illumine the teaching process, scholarly principles, or enable students and faculty to extend knowledge in a given field and understand their discipline's applications to major issues.

Second, the proposed research should assist in supporting the faculty and students in their scholarly pursuits and strengthen the institution rather than fragment it or drain resources from it. This means that universities should be compensated adequately for their costs, both direct and indirect.

Third, universities have a responsibility to cooperate with the society; they are accountable in numerous ways to the society, whether it be the government or private sector, for their role as critic and analyst. They are generally not staffed nor equipped nor geared to implement recommendations for action on a given time scale. And, most importantly, they must be above any political squabbles resulting from proposed actions to solve a given immediate crisis. For example, some scientists within a multidisciplinary group at a nearby institution have reported on solving the garbage collection problem of a major metropolis. Well, I wonder about this on two grounds: The garbage collection problem of that city is far from solved, as observation will indicate. Second, to what extent has this application of essentially old technology contributed to the educational efforts of that institution? Should the university be concerned with this type of issue or rather with developing methods applicable by an operational entity, a city department in this instance, to solving a labor-management-political problem.

Now, this discussion of the academic research arena shows that this is not a new dilemma. These problems arose mainly out of World War II and have leapt in quantum fashion with the huge increase in funding for research and development. Schools, such as M.I.T., established separate entities allied to the parent institution, and didn't worry for many years about whether these appendages contributed to institutional educational and research goals. Other kinds of justification were enough! But universities have tried very hard in the past several years to make sure that the programs they retained contributed to the educational functioning of that institution as opposed to serving a specific problem-solving function such as developing the next missile or biological weapon.

This, then, is what I perceive as the role of our academic institutions. I believe many of them are trying to find the high path over which to travel. A balance must be struck somewhere between the purists who will not soil their hands with any form of application and those activists who would take the university into the marketplace. However, it's a very difficult task to move the members of academia, especially the entrenched faculty.

CRAIG DECKER: Dr. Nash, I think probably everybody is familiar with the Peter principle, which says that professionals tend to rise to the level of their incompetency. A more recent principle, which may be a little tongue-in-cheek but which may have some merit, is the Paul principle. So, if you believe the Peter principle, why hasn't the system fallen apart already? The Paul principle says that the reason it hasn't is that women have been held back and so they haven't had the opportunity to rise to their level of incompetency! Therefore, women are holding the system together. What is your reaction to that principle?

DR. NASH: I'll have to try and decode the message that goes beyond the question. I do feel that what I want to do in my own professional career is to try and maintain this sense of being an outsider at the same time that I perform as a social scientist. I never want to feel so much a part of the establishment that I have to defend every part of it before the outside world. I want to cultivate that awareness in my own work of what it is to be studied as well as to study. My paper was not directed at any specific demands, but asked that all of us as social scientists be aware of how we participate in the process of both collecting and analyzing data. We should be aware of our personal perspective. I don't think that women are going to revolutionize the world. As they become more and more participant in affairs they will lose that very outside awareness that gives them a special advantage at this point. But, as I said, it is a liminal stage and I expect that we may lose that if we aren't careful. I would rather see the awareness spread so that all social scientists are aware of the human motivational factors that enter into their professional statements.

SCIENTISTS IN THE COURTROOM AND THE DEVELOPMENT OF PUBLIC INTEREST LAW

Charles Halpern*

Council for Public Interest Law
Washington, D.C. 20036

In the past several years, American courts have heard cases brought by new kinds of litigants—for example, environmentalists, consumer groups, prisoners, and ex-mental patients. Frequently, they are represented by lawyers associated with public interest law firms. For the past five years, I practiced law with two of these firms, the Center for Law and Social Policy and the Mental Health Law Project. Our primary role was to bring new voices and new constituencies into the legal process—to assist previously unrepresented groups to assert their rights through courts and administrative agencies.

In many cases public interest lawyers have had to find scientific experts who can provide the necessary expert basis on which courts and administrators can make judgments. To our surprise, public interest law practice has frequently led into technologically and scientifically sophisticated areas. For example, public interest litigation has involved the ecological impact of toxic pesticides, the safe disposal of nuclear wastes, the appropriate uses of electroshock therapy, and the efficacy of prescription drugs. Public interest lawyers often found themselves acting as mediators or "translators" between scientists on the one hand and judges on the other.

In one case handled by the Center for Law and Social Policy, environmental groups sought an injunction delaying the construction of an oil pipeline across Alaska.† In order to understand the environmental implications of that project, the lawyers had the awesome task of educating themselves, as well as judges and administrators, in about twenty-five different disciplines. They had to have access to the expertise of men of science such as geologists, biologists, and zoologists.

In another case, involving a defectively manufactured wheel used on pick-up trucks, we needed metallurgists to explain problems in stress and design.‡ In a case challenging a psychosurgery experiment, which I'll discuss at greater length, we had to find neurosurgeons, psychiatrists, neurologists, and others to help us to understand the problem and make it comprehensible to a judge who had to make a decision that interwove science, public policy considerations, and constitutional law.§

Public interest lawyers have had serious problems in finding scientists who will advise us and will testify in court in the wide variety of cases in which scientific expertise is critical. I shall describe our experience in one instance—a case involving psychosurgery. The case illustrates the problem and sheds some light on the factors that I believe lead to our difficulties in finding scientists to participate in the litigation process.

Psychosurgery is a term which refers to a loosely defined cluster of neurosurgical

---

* At the time of the conference, Mr. Halpern was an attorney with the Center for Law and Social Policy and the Mental Health Law project, Washington, D.C. This article was prepared from Mr. Halpern's notes and a transcript of his presentation.
† *Wilderness Society* v. *Morton*, 479 F.2d 842, cert. denied 411 U.S. 917 (1973).
‡ *United States* v. *General Motors*, —— F.2d —— (dec. Aug. 4, 1975, U.S. App. D.C.).
§ *Kaimowitz* v. *Dept. of Mental Health*, 2 Prison L. Rep. 443 (Aug. 1973).

procedures designed to alter behavior that is objectionable either to the subject or to those who have to deal with him. It is a highly controversial technique. In 1972, a group of psychiatrists and brain scientists at the Lafayette Clinic in Detroit developed a research design involving psychosurgery on a dozen involuntarily confined mental patients in state mental institutions. The project had been approved after going through the processes of scientific review within the Lafayette Clinic, including review by special committees empanelled for this experiment. The experiment was about to begin when a group of Michigan citizens filed a suit challenging the constitutionality of the experiment. They argued that the performance of psychosurgery on involuntarily confined mental patients violated the patients' constitutional rights and that such patients could not give a legally valid consent to the procedure. Clearly, this is a case that mixed constitutional and scientific considerations. The constitutional issues could not be resolved until some judgments had been made about the science. How adequate was the scientific design? What is the scientific status of psychosurgery? Is it an experimental procedure? What are the risks to the patient in psychosurgery and what benefits can reasonably be expected? How adequate is the published literature on psychosurgery?

The Mental Health Law Project undertook to study this matter on behalf of the American Orthopsychiatric Association, which entered the case as a friend of the court explicitly to assist the court with the scientific side of this problem. There has been some precedent in recent years for professional and scientific organizations to enter cases as friends of the court to provide scientific expertise. We first had to enlist physicians and scientists to participate in the litigation—to steer us through the mountains of ambiguous literature about psychosurgery, and to help us to evaluate conflicting scientific claims. More difficult still was to find experts who would be willing to go to Detroit, to sit in a courtroom, and to subject themselves to the rather disagreeable process of testifying.

There were three kinds of responses we received from potential advisers and witnesses. The first group, and by far the largest, had a fraternal perspective on the whole matter. They did not want to get involved with a court challenge to what they considered a matter properly resolved within the scientific and medical fraternity. The second group, somewhat more helpful to us, was sympathetic and willing to meet with us; but they were not willing to have their names used or to identify themselves in public. The third category, which was the smallest, agreed to testify.

Finally, after hearing all the expert testimony, the court issued an order prohibiting experimental psychosurgery on involuntary patients in Michigan's mental hospitals.

Cases of this kind are likely to become more common, as groups of citizens challenge the legality of activities affecting their interests which involve sophisticated science. Such challenges will always raise commingled legal and scientific questions. It is essential that courts are adequately informed on the scientific considerations before reaching a decision. I cite this case because it exemplifies the difficulty that we have had in finding expert witnesses to participate in adversary proceedings involving scientific issues. This is typical, and not exceptional.

Why is it that public interest lawyers so often have difficulty in obtaining scientific assistance and advice? I think there are five main factors.

First, in situations in which large corporate interests are involved, we found that many scientific disciplines are dominated by the corporate interests themselves. Finding a metallurgist who knows something about automobiles to testify in court against General Motors, for example, is a very difficult task indeed.

Second, the scientific community has a very negative attitude toward courts' and lawyers' interference in scientific matters. Many scientists consider courts inappropriate institutions to resolve such issues. Rather, scientists feel that these issues should be decided within the scientific community through the peer review process or in the process of obtaining grants. These are some of the obvious ways in which some control is exerted over what scientists do, and the scientific community believes this to be adequate. Compounding this feeling of the inappropriateness of judicial resolution is the view that courts are clumsy and slow, and that too often judges are not only uneducated on scientific matters but uneducable.

A related attitude among many scientists reflects the belief that a scientist who appears in court becomes an advocate and is thereby a less objective scientist. He is branded as an "activist," one who goes outside of scientific channels in order to pursue social policy objectives. It is my impression that scientists do not cherish this role. In the psychosurgery case we relied heavily on the testimony of a neurosurgeon who, for his pains, was subjected to very considerable pressure from his colleagues.

Third, there is the matter of money. The kind of scientific participation in advocacy and consulting which I am discussing typically does not carry with it generous consultant fees; it usually involves no fee at all. This is not an incentive to scientists, particularly in view of the substantial amount of time that may be involved.

Fourth, our courts are built on an adversary process, and testimony in court can be a very unpleasant experience. The lawyers helping scientists to prepare testimony will insist that the scientists grossly oversimplify everything they know. They will do so even to the point, the scientist will feel, of distortion; but this is the part of the lawyer's job as translator. The opposing lawyer on cross examination will highlight the areas of overstatement and incomplete knowledge in the scientist's testimony. The better the lawyer, the more disagreeable will be the experience.

Finally, it is difficult to get help from scientists because of the poor communications that exist between lawyers and the scientific community. Public interest lawyers and the citizen groups they represent often don't know who to talk to, and don't know how to ask questions in the right ways.

This communication problem suggests a possible role for scientific academies. Academies lik the New York Academy could play an important part in facilitating communications between scientists, judges and lawyers. Furthermore, academies could help to legitimize within the scientific community the scientist's role in adversary proceedings.

Courts will, in coming years, continue to deal with cases in which legal and scientific considerations are interwoven. Indeed, the courts have an obligation to pass on the legal claims raised in a case like the psychosurgery case. In this process they will necessarily have to make decisions on highly technical matters. The scientific community should assure that all parties to such proceedings have access to competent scientists to assure that the final decisions are soundly based on a foundation of scientific fact.

These observations regarding science in the courtroom apply with equal force to administrative agencies and the Congress. Citizen groups and public interest lawyers will increasingly participate in deliberations on issues in these forums in which scientific considerations are substantial—and they will look to the scientific community for advice and guidance. Scientists and lawyers should be working out mechanisms to assure that such advice is available.

A MODEST PROPOSAL FOR THE RENAISSANCE OF REGIONAL ACADEMIES OF SCIENCE

Philip Siekevitz

The Rockefeller University
New York, New York 10021

All of us have heard of the National Academy of Sciences, and at least those of us who are here know of the existence of The New York Academy of Sciences, but I think that few of us know that practically every state in the union has an entity called an academy of science. Some are quite old, and even predate the establishment of the National Academy, particularly those in the original thirteen states. These early institutions had as one of their original aims that of promoting "useful knowledge" for the developing technologies of the era, but it quickly became apparent that in order to do this they would have to act as a gathering place for the "natural philosophers" of the day. Thus they began to perform the highly useful role of attempting to organize and to promote research, provide avenues of publication, disseminate information through public lectures, writings, and public natural history collections, and to serve as social and intellectual centers where men and women could meet and exchange ideas. In the eighteenth and nineteenth centuries these academies were active participants and some were even leaders in the establishment of a new order, an order based on scientific technology, and attuned to the social and economic values of the day. They thus served as scientific societies, as publishing houses, as public information groups, even as natural history museums, and as social centers for the innovators of this new order, all these functions being provided for under one roof. Only a few of this type of academy survives to this day; I could mention the Academy of Natural Sciences in Philadelphia, the California Academy of Science in San Francisco, and the Chicago Academy of Science. For with the exponential growth of science in the twentieth century, many of the functions of the early academies were taken over; the "natural philosopher" became extinct, to be replaced by specialists, and thus separate and specific scientific societies were founded, publishing houses were established, and separate natural history and technology museums were set up. As these roles were taken over, the academies began to lose their functions and have retained mostly only one, that of providing a meeting place for discussion among local scientists and that of providing limited publication facilities for these discussions. Some of the academies have proved to be quite successful in this regard, as witness the American Academy of Arts and Sciences in Boston and our own New York Academy of Sciences. However, most of these regional academies became quite limited institutions, performing a very limited role; they had become "small" science in an era of "big" science. This very limited historical survey leads me to my theme: that there is a need for these regional academies, that there is a vital role that they can perform, and that some of them did once perform, a role that is outside the province of the National Academy of Sciences and outside the scope of national scientific societies.

We have heard recently the student cry, "Science for the People," and have been shocked sometimes into unthinking opposition in response to its vehemence. But in calmer moments we must admit that the early academies were really purveyors in their day of "science for the people," for they were almost evangelical in spreading the glories of the new science and the new technology among the public and, in their own view, for the benefit of the public. Their members did not consider themselves as specialists and thus they were not adverse to meeting on an equal nonprofessional basis with whomever might be interested in what they said and what they did. They talked and lectured to anyone who would listen, their fellow natural philosophers, legislators, influential men in commerce, people on the streets. Their motive might be described as a "popularization" of science, for they realized that without public understanding and public support, their vision of a new technological order had little chance of being instituted. And they were successful; their degree of success can be ascertained by just observing the world about us. Of course, the attainment of our technological society is not solely due to the role played by the local academies of science, but I would guess they did have a hand in bringing it about.

As with many other endeavors, the attainment of the goal resulted in a partial dissolution of the enterprise, and the end product is the present morbidity of the local scientific groupings. Another result, influenced by that great agent of change, war, in our case the Civil War, was the establishment of the National Academy of Science. "Little science" was making way for "big science," and some, but by no means all, of the earlier functions of the local academies of science were being taken over by the National Academy. The National Academy was the scientific consultant to government, and as the funding for science was becoming more and more centralized in the federal government apparatus, this meant that the federal government was the recipient of scientific advice. Since, also, it became apparent that the results of scientific research were of immense benefit to the maintenance of an industrialized society, with all its scientific, technical, social, and economic underpinnings, then the role of a central government academy was self-evident. Thus another function of the early regional academies was lost, and to this day only a few, as for example, the Maryland Academy of Sciences, the Chicago Academy of Sciences, the California Academy of Science, and the Southern California Academy of Sciences, offer any consultant service, not to the federal government, but to their regional governmental bodies, although the California Academy of Sciences does cooperate with some agencies of the federal government. I might add that this loss is not entirely the fault of the regional academies, for in many cases, the local or state governments have not availed themselves of offered consultantship facilities, as for example the case of the Ohio Academy of Science and the State of Ohio.

Another function lost by the regional academies has been that of providing public information and education. This was inevitable due to the growth of the communications media: The general public learns of what is going on in science today not from the existing academies but from science reportage in some newspapers and magazines, from a very few radio and TV programs, and from specialized magazines such as *Scientific American*. Of course, there are public lectures within the academies, but they are limited in scope and in audience appeal; except for a few instances, where an academy has also taken on museum functions, the educated public has even forgotten the existence of this possible source of scientific information. They read of great events, of "breakthroughs" in the national news sources, but there is no local organization to which they can go for further explanation. But even in this day of a certain public disenchantment with science and its by-products, there exists a public awareness of the importance of science in our society and a public clamor for more information. David Perlman, the Science Editor of the *San Francisco Chronicle,* describes a series of lectures on cosmic and biological evolution held in San Francisco; the organizers had qualms about fill-ing a 500-seat auditorium, but they had to change the site, for eventually a total of 26,000 people showed up for the series of six lectures. It is instructive that these lectures were sponsored by the NASA, by the Astronomical Society of the Pacific, and by local educational institutions, but not by the local academy of sciences. Here assuredly is a role, not a new role, but a revitalization of an abandoned function for regional academies of sciences.

I have written of what has been lost. Is it worthwhile to try to rejuvenate these regional academies? Or is it better to let them die in their slow lingering ways, realizing that whatever reason for their existence in the past, those reasons no longer hold in a world where science and technology are the greatest progenitors of change. My answer is that, for scientific and social reasons, these local academies can and should be revitalized.

There has been a great deal of commotion recently toward bringing governmental bureaucracies back to within the reach of the people they serve. The feeling is one of lack of rapport, of lack of personal attribution, of a lack of responsiveness, of a feeling that if only there were smaller entities, locally based, these entities would have firsthand knowledge of the problems of people they ostensibly serve, and that these local entities could be made responsive, pressured if you will, much more easily than could distant bureaucracies. Of course, often this is not the case, it is the national body that will be more amenable to people's wishes than will the local political groups. But the feeling is there that government bureaus that make regulations, dispense money, and that set tones and manners, are too distant, and that there are many local problems, even in this jet age, that get lost in national concerns, problems which can get sympathetic hearings only from local officials. And since many of our problems today are of scientific and technological concern, if not of origin, there should be local organizations which can respond to these concerns.

What I am initially suggesting is that the local academies provide and help organize lecture series for the public. The topics can be almost anything, ranging from immediate environmental concerns, through esoteric ones of molecular biology, to how the present social-value system directs the kind of science that is done. As for the esoteric topics, I would venture to say that we scientists consistently underestimate the degree of curiosity, and even of rudimentary knowledge, of lay people, and that we will be surprised at the eagerness of our lay listeners and the magnitude of their attendance. As for the former, the major topics sould certainly be ones which are of concern to urban societies. Where are now forums for public, not "expert," discussion of the uses and misuses of energy, of the advantages and disadvantages of various energy sources, be they oil or nuclear fission? Where are held public discussions on different modes of urban transportation? These forums are not very widespread, I would answer. I could also add that because of a lack of this type of communication, other groups, scientists' information groups, have been virtually forced to organize themselves to provide the information to an eager public. I mention, nationally, the Scientists' Institute for Public Information, and locally, here in New York City, the Scientists' Committee for Public Information. As for other topics, I would suggest that scientists have been more than lax in presenting to a lay audience what goes on in their laboratories. We think that the methodology is so complex, the nomenclature and terminology so esoteric, that it is inconceivable that persons who are not scientists can understand. I beg to differ, for I think any complex topic can be reworded, can be reordered so that persons not at all familiar can understand the principles and the conclusions. It takes a little work on all our parts, but considering the descending nature of the state of public esteem into which we are falling, it is well worth the effort. Basic research can be made understandable to those who wish to learn what is going on in our laboratories, and I think that we would all be surprised at the number of persons who are eager to learn. I am therefore advocating that the local academy of science disperse research and technologic information since its members, scientists of different specialities and persuasions, "experts," if you will, in various fields, constitute a source of public information that can be drawn upon without too much difficulty. And finally, we can educate the public as well as ourselves by holding public seminars on the role of science in society, on the historical perspectives that have led to the present uses of science, on who pays for and who benefits from our science, and on the intimate relationship between the social and political values of society and the kind of science it is willing to support.

Let me be more specific and talk about The New York Academy of Sciences. As many of you know, it has an excellent ongoing conference program, not only for its members, but for all outsiders, including scientists from all over the world. Further, any scientist who cannot attend these conferences can read the proceedings of them in the excellent series, the *Annals*. This is one of the few institutions in the world where conferences are being continually organized and held on any scientific topic. These conferences were in existence and in high esteem when I started in science some twenty-five years ago, and their value has continued to remain high. Because there are few other institutions that have such an ongoing conference schedule, on every aspect in science, these conferences should be continued at these high levels. The Academy also consists of twenty scientific Sections, ranging from Anthropology to Physiology, Engineering, and Science and Public Policy. Most of these sections hold meetings once a month, with invited speakers, so that practically every evening of the academic year, there is one, or even more, scientific meeting going on, attended mostly by scientists in the immediate environs. What I am trying to point out is that The New York Academy serves its scientific members quite well. They can attend conferences and section meetings; they can obtain some of the *Annals* of the Academy free of charge, and others at very low prices; they can publish papers in the *Transactions* of the Academy; they receive monthly a popular magazine, *The Sciences,* which brings them up to date, at a basic level, on some of the branches of science with which they have very little acquaintance. All in all the local scientific community is fortunate to have such an organization in its midst. But I am not here to praise the Academy for those accomplishments; I would rather point out some other, newer directions, which are a necessity in this age. As I mentioned before, the service that the Academy provides is perhaps somewhat outmoded, or at least duplicated, for, as we all know, many conferences are being held, sponsored by a slew of relatively newly arisen societies and institutions, although not on as regular a basis as the Academy's conferences; many other scientific journals and books are published; and many other meetings are held. The functions of the Academy have been taken over, so to speak, by the new specialist organizations, and new roles for the Academy should be sought that these latter institutions cannot provide.

Because of the very geographic location of The New York Academy, these functions must have a local basis. I would group these roles into three categories: informational or educational, consultant or advisory, and advocacy. I have already mentioned the informative role, but let me broaden it a bit. Chautauqua-type lecturers to the general public on scientific topics may be all right, and still necessary, but might it not be too late? By the time adulthood is reached, scientific ignorance is widespread, and any information given to adults is most probably viewed by them as entertainment, of the "gee whiz!" variety. Now New York City and its suburbs have an extensive public school system in which something called "Science" is taught. I do not know what goes into these courses and into the textbooks that are used. Why cannot the Academy try to get into the school-science information field by acting as consultant, through its extensive and variegated membership, to the City and suburban boards of education? Despite the high-school science curricula programs of, for example, the American Institute of Biological Sciences, constant attention is necessary at a local level. We should like to see that the principles of scientific investigation are taught, that scientific results are correctly and clearly expounded, and that the effects, both good and bad, of science and technology on the culture are discussed. We should like to see these topics discussed in relationship to the technological impact on the New York metropolitan area. We should like to see them discussed in relationship to the social and economic policies that affect science itself. Depending on the conditions of the curriculum, perhaps the members of the Academy can even devise basic courses for the various sciences. I do not look upon this venture as merely a propaganda device, to get the children "on our side" when they are young and susceptible, and to be on our side, as adults, when societal priorities are discussed. Rather, the venture should be looked upon as educational: In a world in which science and technology are of utmost importance, it is necessary, if we wish to continue to live in a decent world, in a democratic society, that decisions dependent upon scientific technology be made not only by experts, but also by those who will be most affected—the electorate. Moreover, the electorate should know how and by whom scientific decisions are made, scientific goals are set, and funding is provided. The Academy should begin a process of scientific education in the schools for its own selfish interests, for there cannot exist a free science, in a free society, unless the people know something of what it is all about. This is a part of what "science for the people" is really about, for it is truly, although not solely, "science by the people." It is true that the day of the scientific amateur is past, but scientific decisions can be arrived at by knowledgeable scientists with the aid of knowledgeable amateurs. Let me give a current example: I do not think that the mode of energy usage, its production and conversion, can be arrived at solely on scientific and technological grounds. The economic and social ramifications are so great, affecting all of us, that other viewpoints must be sought. But these other viewpoints, those of the public sectors, if they are to be valid, must derive from a good understanding of the technology involved. And this understanding can only come from information, and the best source of this information is the educational process in our schools.

A second role for the Academy is that of acting as a consultant or advisor, particularly in those local situations where the national interests are not paramount. Why should the national interest, be it through governmental agencies or the National Academy of Sciences, concern itself with the peculiar transportation, housing, or social problems of a singular metropolitan area such as New York City? My answer is that they should not, except, of course, for providing monies, nor are they able to. As far as I know, the extensive scientific and technological knowledge of the Academy, through its members, has never been tapped by New York City or State. For examples, our Atmospheric Sciences and Environmental Sciences sections have never been asked to look at air or water pollution in our city or the effects of highway construction on air pollution; our Biological and Medical Sciences section has never been invited to examine drug-related problems or slum-related disease problems in the city, or the medical care and nutrition problems of the poor; our Computer and Information Sciences section has never been requested to review the ways the city bureaucracies handle their books; our Engineering section has never been asked to examine the various feasibilities outlined, for example, in the West Side Highway Project; our Linguistics section has never been asked to look into bilingual education in our schools; our Psychology section has never been invited to look at the many behavioral problems endemic to an urban environment; our Physical Sciences section has never been asked to evaluate the feasibility of building a small research nuclear reactor on the Columbia University campus; and our Science and Public Policy section has never been asked to look into the general area of how scientifically-derived decisions impinge upon the welfare of the city's inhabitants, or generally how funding for research and development can lead to results whose social and political implications seem far removed from what may be called the general interest. Of course I enumerate all these examples to illustrate that a wealth of scientific knowledge exists, waiting to be used not only by local governmental agencies, but also by many local citizen groups that have sprung up recently to make sure that their interests are not by-passed by decisions arrived at without their consent or even their knowledge. In many regions these local groups have no one to turn to whenever they seek some "expert" advice or solution to some technological problem in order to counter the conclusions presented by the "experts" at the service of the government. Fortunately, here in New York City such a group does exist, the Scientists' Committee for Public Information, but good as their services have been, they cannot draw upon the great wealth of scientific and engineering information that is available to the Academy. Furthermore, the existence of this local group is an unusual situation, not encountered in many other localities in the country. Thus, here is a very important function for local academies, for in many cases these local citizens' groups have nowhere to turn for advice or information; the local academy would be performing a real service by being able to provide, from its membership or from its local contacts, persons willing to do this task. In short, I advocate a sort of "scientific ombudsman" role for the local academy, to serve to allay the citizen's anxieties concerning some technological problem, to serve as a consultant to these people, or even as an adversary against rulings of local bureaucracies and power groups when these rulings may be detrimental to the people ostensibly served.

With respect to the New York Academy, its Sections and their members can serve as more than monthly confreres; these members of the Academy can begin to assume other roles, derived from their field of specialization. Should advice be sought by some local governmental or local citizens action group, shunt the problem over to one of the Sections and let its' members begin to tackle it. I think we would all be surprised by the alacrity with which many of our members, particularly our younger colleagues, would grasp at the opportunity to try to fit their own scientific speciality into its social context. If it is relevance we want, this is a good place to begin. Even in a personal sense, I sometimes feel ashamed that there is something I should do with my knowledge and research besides adding a little bit of knowledge to the future culture of our civilization; I feel that my teaching and research is not enough, and that I owe a bit more to our present culture. This proposed role of the Academy is not a small thing numerically: of our 25,000 members, 2,200 live in New York City and 2,800 more live in the metropolitan area; 5000 social and physical scientists and engineers constitute a wealthy source of available and variegated advice, much of it of high quality.

My final point is one of advocacy, by which I really mean initiative. Our previously mentioned roles as providers of information and as consultants mean that we must objectively *inform,* but we cannot *urge.* However, once we do begin to examine the problem brought before us, solutions can often be devised which ought to be applied before the problems themselves become almost insoluble. At this point it is possible to actively advocate the implementation of these solutions. We can even do so in a limited political sense, for as long as the Academy does not spend more than 10% of its time and resources in a political role, we cannot negate our "holy" tax-exempt status. So, even if our services have never been sought by local governmental agencies in evaluating the problems mentioned above, there is no reason why our Sections cannot start on some of these projects, finish them, and come up with a report that will advocate one approach over the possible others. Indeed, if the Academy wishes to go ahead with the consultantships I have mentioned, the best way to start, in order to gain attention, would be on our own. There is no dearth of problems and I believe there is no dearth of interested and dedicated talent in the Academy; all that is needed is direction and will.

Not quite all; for there always arises the problem of "paying the piper." What can be tapped are the ongoing sources of funds: governmental agencies and foundations. The National Science Foundation has a Public Understanding of Science Project; so far as I know no academy has yet attempted to become a participant in that program. Indeed, the NSF itself and a committee of the Federal Council for Science and Technology (FCST) both recommended additional funding for an NSF program that helps states and cities set up their own science advisory apparatus, as well as funding for a variety of programs to set up applied R & D and technology utilization programs in local settings. It would be comparatively easy for local academies to come in under this umbrella, especially when the report of the FCST concludes that "state and local governments stand, with respect to the utilization of science and technology, roughly where the federal government did in 1940." In the case of disease-related projects, the Department of Health, Education and Welfare can be approached; in the case of environmental problems, the Environmental Protection Agency is there with the money. However, the bulk of the funding for any of the projects I have mentioned would probably have to be local since the problems are local, and the advocated solutions would utilize local resources. I know that the cities are broke, but not so broke to deny funding to a project whose solution may save the city much more than it has invested in its solution. And the expense would not be great; the labor is free, so that this substantial portion of costs can be disregarded. Furthermore, the overhead would provide a small source of funds for the Academy, an additional one over that provided by membership, donations, and publications. I think the Academy would benefit, not least by public esteem and membership satisfaction; the city would benefit, since it could attain a high-grade consultantship advice almost at cost. Indeed why should the city have to seek out private organizations like the Rand Corporation of New York to give scientific and technological advice, when an organization already exists that can draw on a much greater source of scientific knowledge and technological evaluation? Even as a last resort, why cannot the New York Academy use its own funds for such projects? It will be its own piper and play its own tunes. It will truly be an independent organization, serving the whole public, and not beholden to those wielding the money.

So, I present the foregoing ideas to The New York Academy of Sciences, hoping that some of these ideas might be very soon put into force. Perhaps other academies of science can do likewise; perhaps the success of even a single project by the New York Academy will be a goad for other academies to do likewise. For it is a pity that in many cases the skeletal organizations of local scientists exist, ready to be filled out with the "muscle" of doing a public service. This was once one of the functions of local academies of science, and it can be restored. In this day of national "big science," "little science" can not only still thrive, but also can actually fill a necessary role for the continuation of scientific endeavor in a democratic society. The integrity and independence of the local academies of science need not be circumscribed a bit; indeed, it is those very qualities that will make the functions of the academies useful to all segments of society—those with power and those without power.

Finally, should the local academies of science undertake all these functions, they should do so with a feeling of humility. We scientists do not have all the answers, and even within our own scientific specialities, our answers are only partial ones. Also, science and technology are but one input into the workings of our society. Our advice and our recommendations are therefore only one aspect within the total purview of those who must make the decisions in our democratic society. We should forcibly put them forward, but we should not insist on them, for in some cases our recommendations should not be followed if society is to be ultimately benefited. We should not be discouraged, for is it not in the methodology of science that we go by steps towards solutions, and that at any one point we might have taken a wrong step? We might be in error in our advice, given the tentative nature of our knowledge, but in all humility, we could add that our judgements may be less prone to error than those of others. Keeping this perspective in mind, we can add something good and useful to our local areas, and by that, possibly contribute to the welfare of the whole nation.

GENERAL DISCUSSION

DR. STEVEN ROSE: Dr. Siekevitz has given us a coherent and practical set of statements about what is to be done, and that really ought to be the end point of this meeting, but I will attempt to summarize what has gone before and I will try to end on a comparably optimistic and humble note. I shall not attempt to go over as a whole the very complex ground that we went over during the course of the day. Some of the things I shall have to say may disagree with remarks made by some of our other speakers. You should not expect a wholly impartial summary from me, and therefore the opportunity for discussion is to be welcomed. In fact, this meeting has been remarkable for the degree and intensity of the discussion it has provoked. The seriousness with which not only the speakers but also the listeners and discussants have taken the very many issues that have been raised is a positive attribute in terms of the dynamics of the entire meeting. We have gone over a great deal of territory and many hairs have been raised. Issues have ranged from the very grainy, practical questions of the financial base of scientific activity to questions of much more ideological significance. I want to try to do justice to both these stands.

We started the day with Dr. Creutz talking about the structure of decision-making within the National Science Foundation; how money was allocated; and how he saw decision-making processes operating from his vantage point. I disagreed with him somewhat at that point as to whether this represented a truly democratic process of decision-making rather than an elite process.

Dr. Roth then spoke on the need to address ourselves to the question of universities and medical institutions. He made a plea, which is a familiar one to an English person, that you at least preserve some institutions within the structure that are not going to be tied to short-term responsibilities and mission-oriented work. He believes that the universities can and should serve this more long-term function.

Then Dr. Friedman talked about the American Chemical Society and the role of concerned professionals in the context of a decision-making structure, and he suggested ways in which they could influence these processes and how their members might serve.

In a long and illuminating account Dr. Henry David* warned of the limitations and described the structure of advice-making and advice-giving. All these speakers represent one strand of thought that can be picked out of today's discussions. I will come back to the second strand later.

I want to examine this particular strand because it makes certain assumptions at the micro level about who is actually making the decisions, who is giving the advice, and in whose interests they serve. In terms of the question of the nature of advice within the National Academy of Sciences, I was reminded of a point Patrick Blackett made before he became a very respectable president of the British Royal Society. In a book that he published around 1945 with a group of other radical scientists called *Science and the Nation* he said that we have no time for those of our scientific colleagues who are so frightfully scientific—they don't know on which side they stand. The fact of the matter is that scientists *do* take sides, even when they don't seem to, and Dr. David was very clear that this was the case. I was sorry that Dr. David didn't point to the very sharp questions that have been

---

* It is regretted that Dr. David's manuscript was not received in time for publication in this *Annal*.

posed within the National Academy itself on the herbicide study, and I'm sorry he neglected to cite the positions taken by Drs. Levins and Lewontin, who, in one case resigned from the Academy and in the other refused election to the Academy. Each man felt the incompatibility between the role of being an elite advisor to the state while at the same time disagreeing with so many aspects of governmental policy. This is the key point in our discussion today. Time and again we've come up against the problem of the extent of the social responsibility of the scientist. Is it the job of the scientist to advise the state even though he feels the state is unlikely to take his advice or even though he generally is in profound disagreement with many aspects of governmental policy or the structure of society? Or is it his job instead to go out and work with those groups within society to which he finds himself politically committed? I ask these questions because there is a tension between the *advocacy* role that Mr. Halpern was talking about and the *advisory* role that incorporates the scientist within the structure of the state. There is a clear disjunction between those who make one decision and those who make the other.

Mr. Halpern discussed this problem with particular reference to psychosurgery, but he pointed to the general difficulty in getting scientists to come out and commit themselves publically in a political controversy such as the kind raised by the question of psychosurgery.

Here I would like to note something that never fails to impress me greatly when I come to the United States as a visitor from Britain: And that is that I don't think people outside the States recognize the tremendous power of advocacy and aggressive legal action of the sort that surrounds such issues as psychosurgery. You recognize here that the law can be used as an instrument for actually extending the rights of the citizens of this country. This is something for which we lack a system or technique in Britain, where legal activities for those out of joint with society are much more concerned with defensive action, rather than the positive and creative ways to which the legal process is put to use here.

Coming back to Mr. Halpern's point that he found it difficult to find scientists who were prepared to be advocates: That is instructive, because all that we've heard during the course of this conference is indeed how scientists are advocates. They are extremely skillfull and articulate when arguing for their own scientific interests and when petitioning for more money for this, more for that, more money for the variety of boondoggles that doubtless Dan Greenberg would have mentioned had he been here. So we see that scientists can be very aggressive and are very well able to argue a case when it is in their interest to do so. And yet, when the time comes, when they are put in a position of coming out in public to argue for protection of a particular group that is threatened within the social structure, as in the psychosurgery case, they are suddenly silent. Those who do stick their necks out and commit themselves often find themselves in some difficulty, as Mr. Halpern pointed out.

We must recognize that for the most part scientists are members of the decision-making elite, and part of the privileged groups within society. And so we find their advice not disinterested, but protective of their own interests, their own needs, and the structures of their own institutions; their advice works to obtain funds for the things that they want. So we shouldn't be too surprised to find that only a limited number among the "scientific community" are prepared to act against the interests of their own professional group by playing the advocacy role, which is so urgently needed. There are certainly enough stock issues in which activity of this sort would be highly desirable. However, in the long run, we have to come to terms with the whole structure of the system, in which even this advocacy role has its limitations.

At this point we come back to Dr. Siekevitz's passionate plea for the public participation in science and for scientists to go out to the people. Meetings of this sort often fail to suggest concrete and practical actions. Consequently, it would seem very desirable for the New York Academy, through its various bodies, to actually debate and consider the actions that Dr. Siekevitz has so specifically enumerated. At the very least such activities can do no harm; at best, they may do a great deal of good.

Finally though, I want to address the other strand of thought that can be found at this meeting. That point was raised by Dr. Nash's presentation. If I may generalize from the very real issues of sexism, particularly in social science and anthropology, Dr. Nash was talking about the structure of scientific knowledge itself—and that is something that we have to come to grips with and can't abandon as irrelevant to the discussion. It seems to me that Dr. Nash was saying that inevitably within the structure of our society scientific knowledge has certain ideological functions. She pointed to the ways in which science, and she used her particular science as an example, ignored women, invalidated them, and regarded them as somehow outside the scope of scientific inquiry. She also raised, fascinatingly and elusively, the question of the very masculine nature of scientific knowledge itself, an issue which certainly needs discussion. Dr. Nash pointed out that the scientific organizations we have been discussing today and yesterday are in some ways masculine structures. They reflect a particular social order in which the male is dominant. If we are to move forward to creating a science of the people, like the open science Dr. Siekevitz was advocating, we have to ask what form that science will take. We cannot assume that it will take the form of the male-dominated science that is practiced now, with all its ideological limitations. If we are opening up science to more than just those women who, as Dr. Nash said, are honorary brothers and honorary males, then we also have to open ourselves to the possibility that the forms that such a people will choose will be very different from science as it is presently structured.

I will end on a positive note which combines the concerns of Dr. Siekevitz, Dr. Halpern, and Dr. Nash. That involves the opening of science to many broader strata in the population, not merely to an elite of experts who come up with the goods, the scientific truth that they actually lay open for the public to comment on and advise upon. That is not the way that it should be. Science, if it is to be a creative and living force and not merely an aspect of the domination of nature and the domination of man, must always be related to the practice and activities of real people—the mass of the people, male and female, working class and nonworking class, black and white, within the context of the society within which we live. If we open out science in terms of its practice, not simply in terms of the clash of expert and counterexpert, to this much broader public criticism, activity, and understanding, then we are really in the business of helping to create a science for the people.

I do not believe that as scientists we can do this ourselves. I believe that this actually can only take place within the context of activity of all the people transforming the structure of the science that we make. There are numbers of positive ways in which we can help; Dr. Siekevitz pointed to some of these. Implicit in Dr. Nash's and Mr. Halpern's remarks were some other suggestions we can use to move forward. When we leave this conference, we who are in scientific practice will do well to ask ourselves how we can actually improve and develop our own practice, our own activities in science, in the direction of opening it up to make it a genuine science for and by the people.

DR. MELMAN: Dr. Siekevitz, in your lucid formulation of the rationality that would prevail if the government of New York City were to use the talents that could be mobilized by The New York Academy of Sciences, one critical feature of the situation was not amplified. It is precisely the possible influence of advice from scientific bodies on matters technical, hence imbued with political, economic, and social considerations, that government administrators and policy-makers fear. They are wary of accepting advice from a large freewheeling, coequal consultant body. Indeed, the attempt by the then-bosses of the Section on Science and Public Policy of this Academy, when John Lindsay was Mayor, to establish the kind of ongoing relationship with the city government that was suggested by Dr. Siekevitz resulted in one of the speediest and most permanent demonstrations of bureaucratic disappearance and withdrawal that I've ever seen. They ran in fright. The lesson here seems to be that precisely the readiness of the city government to have recourse to agencies like the Rand Corporation and other consulting-for-fee groups is associated with the control that necessarily is vested in the receiver of the report from agencies of this type. And that control is ordinarily understood as not being comparably exercised where a city government is to receive reports from such a group as The New York Academy of Sciences. So I suspect that while the consultancy role can and should be advocated, and formulated perhaps in a way that is less threatening to various city administrators, it may very well turn out that if we wish to have increasing input on a number of problems that we're technically competent to deal with and feel that we are politically justified in dealing with, our role will be as advocates with a background of expertise rather than as consultants.

DR. SIEKEVITZ: Let me give an example of one of the problems inherent in consultancy. We all know that New York City is a rapidly turning-over city. Buildings are constantly being torn down and others erected. Frequently the buildings being torn down are tenements or even good apartment houses and in their place office buildings are going up. Consequently, some of the services that are of value to the people in those neighborhoods, such as libraries, firehouses, or police stations, are no longer really necessary in that neighborhood. So the Rand Corporation was asked to look at this problem. One of their solutions was to do away with some of the firehouses and police stations since they weren't affording optimal service and therefore represented a waste of city money. You can imagine the clamor when this conclusion was published. My point, however, is that considerations other than the technological must be taken into account. Just because the police station is an economic loss doesn't mean that we can ignore its contribution to the wellbeing of the people. So, the question of citizen morale would be an overriding concern. These public facilities might be of no utilitarian value, except in a psychological sense. In that sort of study the Rand Corporation should have brought in some psychologists, for example, to predict the consequence to this neighborhood if these services were to be suspended.

The consultantship role then is partially a warning role. It must look at a problem from a different point of view; it must ask a different sort of a question; and it must come up with a different sort of answer or perspective.

DR. DAVID: I'd like to sneak up slightly on some of the things that Steven Rose said. From the vantage point of within the advisory institution I tried to present the different sets of issues from the point of view of a client, the asker, and the receiver of advice. The long and short of the story is that serious, well-considered, well-founded scientific advice on a range of issues that have public policy dimensions tends to be threatening. One of the functions of science is to demythologize. It takes conventional wisdom and conventional ways of looking at the world, both as a physical and a social universe, and says in effect "hey, it ain't so." It says there's no evidence to support your view that people with dark skins are inferior. It says simple notions to explain why blacks looted in Detroit in 1967 don't fit; we've learned something to the contrary. It says that systems of incentives that you propose to use to induce this or that kind of behavior won't work. From the viewpoint of the recipients of advice, asking for it is often like an invitation to suicide. That poses another set of problems that I won't explore now.

Pompideau once remarked that there were three ways for a politician to ruin his career. One is to chase women; a second is to gamble; and the third is to trust experts. He said the first is the most pleasant; the second the quickest; and the third, trusting experts, is the surest way to ruin your career. I mention this because what Dr. Rose spoke of as the structure of knowledge is in itself the most critical thing in forming a view of the world and its problems and solutions. We may do nothing more than rearrange them or reorder their significance.

I want to move from his remarks about the structure of knowledge, which were very pertinent, to the strength of the rhetoric of notions about science for and by the people. I do not know what that phrase means operationally. I understand what it means in terms of enhancing understanding of the world in which people live and why things work that way they do and how things can be explained in some sensible fashion. The interesting thing is that when knowledge is not perturbing or it disturbs only small numbers of people, no one is bothered about accepting the most revolutionary ideas. Black holes are not disturbing, if someone announces their existence. On the other hand, it is disturbing if some scientist announces, whether soundly or not, that his evidence shows a certain differential in performance between ethnic groups can be ascribed to genetic factors. That is profoundly disturbing because some people would prefer to maximize the differential and others would prefer to minimize it. It's not so disturbing if someone tells you that we've identified something on the order of 3,000 genetically-determined diseases. It's very disturbing if you begin to say other things in which the genetic in lieu of performance may or may not be significant.

Science for the people might mean aiding in the comprehension of the nature of human life and experiences and of grappling with the human condition, in both its perfectable and imperfectable aspects. Science by the people gives me pause, however, because we are not sure about its operational manifestation. There are gross inequities in the distribution of knowledge and there are relatively impotent and vulnerable groups in our society who do not have access to or who could not deploy the potential power that knowledge could give them. I find it difficult to go beyond that. If the question is whether we should devote scientific energy to issues that trouble a society, the answer is very strongly yes. If we look at the history of the development of the social behavioral sciences, we see that it has been profoundly shaped by ameliorist impulses. Whole new disciplines have been devised in response to public policy concern, but we haven't shaped public policy by these means. The causal relationship has gone the other way. So, if I were to applaud Dr. Rose's rhetoric, I must ask what it means operationally. I don't think he has in mind a program such as the one Dr. Siekevitz suggested.

DR. ROSE: Henry David, with considerable accuracy and precision, has pointed to the key issue here. What I mean by science by and for the people is different from or more extensive than the advocacy roles suggested by Dr. Halpern or the extensive set of proposals that Dr. Siekevitz made. What I'm trying to say is this: I think that the structure of our scientific knowledge is not divorced from the sort of society in which we live. In an elitist, hierarchical, sexist, racist society we produce science that structures knowledge about the natural world in a way that is elitist, hierarchical, sexist, and racist. In this sense science in a society that has eliminated these characteristics is a different sort of science. A science by the people is a science in fact that is not sexist or hierarchical or racist because it is done by a mass of the people rooted in their own practice, their own experience, and their own activities in the context of this different structure of society. We could offer the example of China as a clue for direction that might be followed in the United States or Britain. Quite clearly each society develops its own paths based on its own national cultural traditions. It is not good enough to assume that a solution adopted in one country can be translated lock, stock and barrel into another. But we can emulate the attempt to bring forth justice and to eliminate the dichotomy between theory and practice and the barrier between expertise and nonexpertise.